GOLD AND SILVER TREASURES OF ANCIENT ITALY

Text by Carlo Carducci

Published by New York Graphic Society

Greenwich, Connecticut, U.S.A.

Library of Congress catalog number 63-22472
Literary and Reproduction rights reserved for all Countries

© 1963 - IN ITALY BY SILVANA EDITORIALE D'ARTE - MILAN - ITALY

Printed in Italy

The Antique Italian Gold and Silver Exhibition opened on June 16, 1961, at the Palazzo Chiablese in Turin. In September of the same year the Exhibition was moved to the Castello Svevo in Bari and later still, to the Museo Nazionale in Naples, where it remained open to the public until its appearance in the Palazzo Reale in Milan. The Exhibition was thus conceived as a travelling showpiece. It was organized by the Direzione Generale alle Antichità e Belle Arti, assisted by the Superintendents and Directors of Italian State and Communal Museums.

About a thousand pieces of jewelry and silver were sent to Turin from all parts of Italy. The intention was to present the evolution of these precious objects as completely as was possible. The exhibition offered not only a spectacle but also demonstrated an implicit desire to solve, or at least to bring to light, questions which remain unanswered about previous civilizations. In the first place the pieces shown were sufficient to stir the imagination of any visitor. Secondly, from a cultural point of view, the Exhibition presented a section of the history of art and civilization on which much research is taking place. The great range of the objects shown comprises elements of historical, social and commercial interest, primarily concerned with the distribution of wealth and fashions in living.

The most valuable products of early goldsmiths have been collected before, but such collections were concerned either with the craft of a particular region, and were therefore too limited, or else their range was so wide as to make any serious documentation impossible. What the organizers of the Turin Exhibition attempted to do was to concentrate, if not on all the gold and silver jewelry found in Italy, at least on that part of it which could be considered as most helpful in assessing the techniques and styles of the many groups in relation to the origin of the products and to the details of their location. Their aim was to identify the areas or centres of production, to assess evidence of trade, commerce and principal lines of traffic and ultimately to establish, on the basis of these elements, a comprehensive chronology.

On the one hand, therefore, the selection and assembly of this jewelry for these purposes should be considered as an illustration of the problem. At the same time it offers general guidance for the more serious studies that have now been acknowledged as indispensable to those who want to become familiar with this particular form of art. In this connection one should remember that the evolution of jewelry, far from being merely a series of works developed by craftsmen, embraces several works which are often true and proper masterpieces executed by highly refined artists.

Many great artists, whose fame is based on their pictorial or sculptural activities, were often described in artistic and literary sources as goldsmiths and jewelers. We should also remember that the evolution of this craft cannot be considered simply as the outward sign of economic prosperity or wealthy ostentation, but must also be regarded as the most obvious judgment of the taste and refinement of a society that chose to express its cult of beauty even in frivolous and short-lived decorative objects.

The Turin Committee published a catalogue of the Exhibition, extensively illustrated with photographs and rich in bibliographical data. It was edited by Dottoressa Finocchi. The introduction, by Professor Amedeo Majuri, provides a scholarly evaluation of the craft, and other introductory articles deal with the various sections included in the Exhibition. The catalogue is, therefore, a scientific work. Both precise and accurate, it is indispensable for a study of this subject. This book is not meant to replace the Exhibition's official catalogue — which remains the most reliable guide — but is aimed at complementing it with a somewhat more specialized description of the objects on show; it draws attention to technical details in certain objects. In this book, space has been largely given over to the more precise and acute eye of the camera which, by interpreting the most subtle shades of composition, helps one to understand the extraordinary imagination of the various artists and the superb technique of the craftsmen. There are here approximately a thousand objects of various types and origins, illustrating the development of jewelry from the earliest epoch (8th—7th centuries B. C.) to the so called "late-ancient period", from the Romans to the Barbaric invasions (6th—7th centuries A. D.).

Thus the background is political, economic and social history over fifteen centuries. This comprises the Etruscan civilization — rich in Oriental associations; the Celtic civilization in Italian provinces which were longest dominated by the Gauls; the culture of Sardinia with its many Phoenician and Punic influences; the great centres of Sicily and Magna Grecia echoing the culture of the Western Greeks. The domination of Rome lasted until the beginning of the first crisis of the Roman Empire. Classic civilization dissolved under the new barbaric impetus of the Goths and Lombards who alternated with the Byzantines in ruling Italy.

ETRUSCAN JEWELRY

Etruscan jewelry was represented by 130 items discovered in the areas of Palestrina, Tarquinia, Bisenzio, Vetulonia and Populonia. They are important in that the Etruscans deliberately left them as a record of their hegemony. For them, in fact, and for the

Statue of Venus in gold " bikini " found at Pompei - *Naples, Museo Archeologico Nazionale.*

Lucumones (their elite), the jewel was an outward mark of human dignity. Commerce and wars had brought them into contact with the great Mediterranean markets — dominated by the Punics, Cypriots and Phoenicians — but from the very start they had also defended their territory against the Celtic tribes and stemmed the advance of the first Greek settlers such as the Ionians, and the Phoenicians. One can understand how the Etruscans' production echoes the technical and artistic influences of all the peoples they encountered, with their different origins and traditions.

Two types of production emerge from the great variety of forms and decorative motifs, a native and local production and an imported one. The first group may in its turn be subdivided into a North-central and a South-central area, the former showing a tendency towards a more delicate granulation (see page XXVI), with simple geometrical motifs, and the second one revealing plastic decoration rich in colour and more

Small handle of vase or amphora in gilded bronze, found at Palestrina - *Rome, Museo Villa Giulia.*

Detail of Venus in gold " bikini ".

coarsely granulated — a taste that was to become more clearly defined in the Barbaric era. This distinction, however, is not always evident and one frequently meets with objects and relics of different tastes and fashions which have been found, for example, in a tomb.

Such is the case of the Bernardini tomb, from Preneste. The large clasp (Plate 3) decorated with chimaeras, lions and harpies is of a clearly oriental and baroque inspiration (particularly in the *horror vacui* dominating the distribution of its ornaments). Then we have the smooth drinking cup (Plate 4 a) whose elegant form and restrained decoration is perfect evidence of its early Corinthian origins. The other object found in the same tomb, the small basin in gilded silver (Plate 2) is definitely an imported article, as shown by the Phoenician character of its hammered figures; the composition clearly follows some Egyptian design, and the technique is reminiscent of certain Syrian and Cypriot plates.

The fibula in the Lictor's grave at Vetulonia (Plate 9 b) — which surely originates from the Northern area — shows in its form and style a reaction to the Eastern manner of decoration, even though it reveals the beginning of that difficult, delicate technique of refined, dust-like granulation. This was a marvellous discovery which, through an interplay of tonalities, had the effect of heightening the splendour of the metal.

After its early Eastern phase — its finest period — Etruscan production of jewelry appears to have lost its creative vitality, even though it still had many objects of unique refinement and beauty.

Between the sixth and fifth centuries B. C. the Italiot production of jewelry was given new inspiration by Greece, whose early, somewhat affected Ionian style was shortly to be replaced by the more solid Attic style. But Greece's leadership was not unopposed nor did its influence spread evenly over the vast Tyrrhenian region: many varieties and differences of interpretation are visible to this day, in spite of the obvious uniformity of figuration which is the most typical mark of Greek ascendancy.

Thus in such jewelry from the Northern area one generally sees the hand of a craftsman intent on continuing — though in simplified form — the eclectic tradition of the old linear and classic decorative motifs. These became translated into a technique which Mansuelli aptly describes as " pseudo-granulation " (see the earrings in Plates 10 and 14; the necklace in Plate 13 b). But besides these works, there are others which are more refined and occasionally are even masterpieces. They are more reminiscent of Greek art. An example of this is the Bologna ring (Plate 12) and, in a lesser degree, the Vetulonia bract (Plate 11 a).

A greater measure of refinement was created in the south by the Etruscan civilization coming into contact with Greek culture. This phenomenon is best seen in the Ruvo necklace (Plate 29), decorated with masks of Silenus and acorns. Its execution surpasses even the most sophisticated craftsmanship. Indeed it has a freshness and an originality such as could stem only from a genuine artist. Even though it is not easy to identify the centre of production from which the necklace originated — it has been variously described as Magna Grecia or imported from Etruria — it is obvious that in this ornament Etruscan technique and taste are admirably blended with the restrained configurations of Hellenistic tradition.

By now the representational element had imposed a definite change on Etruscan jewelry. It was no longer pure *decoration,* as during the phase of Oriental influence. Due to a gradual clarifying of form, it had become a *figurative representation.* But another element appears more and more often in the golden body of the jewel: this was the gem. From the marriage of these two elements, equally refined but very different both in shape and colour, a new taste for polychromy was born, and was to become especially prevalent in Roman art.

The Etruscan jewel of the fourteenth century is not easily described. It appears to be generally mass-produced, and often its figurative representation portrays mythical scenes (see the Bomarzo mirror, Plate 15). Single figures or a group of figures are inserted in the lacy-thin texture of the powder spray and of the granulation. Here and there the great decorational themes recur. Although some objects retain undeniable evidence of good taste (see the earrings of Florence and Populonia, Plate 17), generally the decoration becomes more and more mechanical, and the forms richer and more complicated.

The objects found in the Todi tomb, including the gold-mail necklace and the heavy earrings (Plates 19 and 21) are attributed to the mature Greek period. Here, the complicated pattern of loose hanging ornaments and small chains, and the bracts decorated with figures and alternating with seals set with onyx constitute a perfect anthology of Etruscan jewelry during this period.

CELTIC JEWELRY

In the Etruscan section of the Exhibition a whole showcase was reserved for objects found in the Marche area. Outstanding among the many necklaces, rings and earrings, was one particular jeweled ornament. This was the torques, a collar of Celtic origin. Its owner, Titus Manlius, the consul who won the battle of the Aniene, added the title, Torquatus, to his name, for he had seized the collar from a defeated enemy.

The specimen found at Monte Fortino (Plate 16 a), though discovered in a Gallic burial ground, is not truly representative of the torques which the blonde, Junoesque Gallic women wore round their necks. It is more probably a local copy of an ornament which was then becoming fashionable. An original piece is the Filottrano torques (Plate 23 b), massive in shape and decorated as far as the venation of the leaves set

Italiot vase in the form of a woman's head - *Taranto, Museo Nazionale.*

around the terminals. There are other examples of Gallic jewelry which are found only rarely in Italy: a collection of horse-buckles was found at Manerbio (Plate 23 a); they are hammered into thin silver laminae and decorated with typically Celtic motifs, such as the triskele (a symbolic figure consisting of three legs radiating from a common centre), and with isolated heads, surely related to the *têtes coupées* of the Celtic peoples.

The collection from Sardinia is richer: especially items from Tharros, Nora, Sulcis, Cagliari and Olbia. This is an isolated group comprising eclectic forms and decorations with elements and motifs of Punic-Phoenician, Assyrian, Egyptian and Greek

XII

origin. During a period extending from the 8th century B. C. to the late Roman age, Sardinia revealed traces of an early Punic phase dying out about 480 B. C.; a phase of political economic and religious reformation in Carthage (480-490 B. C.); a longer phase embracing the peak of Sardinian civilization with its Alexandrine influences and ending with the Roman occupation of the island (409-238 B. C.).

The period that followed is evidence of how vital the Sardinian traditions remained under the Romans, and how they became enriched by late-Etruscan and Hebrew contributions.

The Sardo-Carthaginian production of jewelry is well represented by an armlet decorated with motifs of Phoenician style; two earrings (Plates 25 a and b) strongly reminiscent of similar ornaments found at Ephesus, Rhodes and Cyprus; and a set of cylindrical boxes containing golden laminae with scenes showing Egyptian influence.

It would be difficult, not to say impossible, to trace some of these motifs — which are themselves an intricate pattern of influences and styles — before they arrived in the Mediterranean island of Sardinia. So far as the Italian mainland is concerned, the most ancient jewels were certainly executed before the arrival of the Greek settlers, and it is not improbable that the rings with the typical " eye-shaped " socket found in the Sicilian necropolis of Pantalica and Caltagirone go back as far as the geometrical Eastern period of the 10th and 11th centuries B. C.

The two specimens from Sant'Angelo Muxaro (Plate 27 b) must belong to the same

Necklace pendants with stamped female heads, from Taranto - *Taranto, Museo Nazionale.*

XIII

type, but many elements lead us to believe that they were made at a later date by Sicilian craftsmen, even though their figuration still bears the marks of Mycenaean tradition.

It is not always easy to record the evolution of jewelry in Magna Grecia and, at least so far as the more ancient periods and the most northern areas are concerned, it is hard to distinguish the typically Greek from the Italiot and Etruscan character.

There are also works which, though found in Greek areas, have retained an Italiot character. In the Ruvo necklace, for instance, we have seen technique, motif and decoration, which are definitely Etruscan in taste.

The examples shown included a yellow amber necklace (Plate 26) with undeniable Etruscan characteristics, found at Cuma in surroundings that were clearly Greek. It was dated between the 8th and 7th centuries B. C. Similarly, a rosette of more or less the same period reveals signs of Rhodes production (Plate 27 a).

So far as the 6th century is concerned, the objects on show comprise some typical balm-containers and a fine pendant from Noicattaro (Plate 31) depicting a lively hare hunt.

The 5th century is represented by few objects and, indeed, in Greece itself few ornaments of this period have been found. This might be explained by the fact that, during the time of the great masters, the Greek laws regulating expenditures forbade the use of jewelry in the adornment of statues; while in Italy, perhaps, there were fewer goldsmith workshops. There appears to be no solution other than that this period was a phase of transition in Magna Grecia, or was at least a period of preparation for forms and motifs that were to develop in the following centuries. Production in the 4th and 3rd centuries B. C. was concentrated around Taranto — the Paris of Magna Grecia — which also became a great centre for the diffusion of jewelry. Here, originality of form and richness of decorative formulas were admirably blended. It was an epoch unrivalled in elegance and refinement. The craftsmen were sophisticated, the artists sincere and stimulated by great creative force. The detail of their delicate work reveals the background of a prosperous, contented society, and an artistic impulse striving for perfection through exuberance of form and splendour of decoration. This, incidentally, is also visible in the rich, flowery style of the painted vases of this period.

Local workshops must have executed the jewels found in graves at Crispiano, Mottola, Ginosa, Roccanova, and in other tombs discovered at Taranto itself or at nearby Manosa. Several of those objects betray an almost extravagant imagination and taste, and the majority were fashioned for women. The head of the ring (Plate 37 b) would be widened to contain, perhaps, a portrait of a woman with a strong nose and fleshy lips; earrings (Plate 35 b) would support bunches of grapes, cones or pyramids, hanging upside down; and the pendants themselves would hold minute figures of cupids, victories, winged horses, maenads and centaurs, swinging from small chains.

The "Knot of Hercules" now appears and becomes fashionable, since it allows the development of spiral-bands and rosettes, and the delicate interplay of filigree branches is completed by pendants and precious acorns. The artist's imagination also found great scope in the ends of bracelets and armlets, which he would decorate with heads of rams and lions. Dolphins became the typical clasp for delicate gold-mail chains.

But the desire to copy nature was revealed especially in the wreath and tiara that had by now replaced the simple gold band of the classic era. A wreath of entwined leaves, flowers, and fruit of various shapes and colours is perhaps as ancient as man himself, but no one ever imparted such grace and beauty to this form as the

Small figure of dancing girl in multi-coloured terracotta, from Taranto - *Taranto, Museo Nazionale.*

Detail of bracelet clasp reproduced in plate 37 a - *Taranto, Museo Nazionale*.

goldsmiths from Taranto. They immortalized the wreath of oak, myrtle, olive and laurel leaves in slim, gold laminae; their roses, after so many centuries, have lost none of their original beauty; the rubies and enamels still retain the iridescent sheen of freshly cut flowers.

ROMAN JEWELRY

The Roman craft developed under the influence of both Greeks and Etruscans. Some scholars point out, as evidence of its originality, specimens of the late Republican period found in Campania (the Naples area); others hold that no genuinely original examples exist before the 3rd century of Imperial Rome. The problem of its beginnings is therefore complex. It is less difficult, however, to subdivide the areas of production and diffusion, especially in the light of geographical location and historical events.

We thus observe that in the southern provinces, contacts with Magna Grecia became closer after the conquest of Taranto by the Romans (272 B. C.) and that immediately afterwards the Greek tradition in jewelry spread to the great markets of Campania.

There is no clear-cut distinction between the jewel in Greek taste and that of Roman manufacture; the same traditional forms appear in each and the same patterns are repeated in a somewhat mechanical, shoddy manner. Probably at the root of this indifferent, unimaginative workmanship wa an industrial and commercial phenomenon, caused perhaps by the increasing demand for jewels even by people with small means.

XVI

Multi-coloured terracotta, from Taranto - *Taranto, Museo Nazionale.*

But at the same time these indifferent works reveal new inspiration — a search for liveliness of colour.

In the central provinces, on the other hand, the art and technique of the Etruscan jewel were constantly progressing. This was not, of course, the Eastern-type jewelry, nor that influenced by the great masters from Greece, but rather the product of a late Italiot style, of modest taste and limited in conception and execution.
Yet a certain search for colour is apparent in these works, particularly in the vibrations of light imparted to the smooth golden surfaces.

In the central northern regions that had had a more protracted Celtic domination the process of Romanization was slower. While the Celtic tribes in the Marche had absorbed the Italiot culture, we find that in the Po Valley and especially in the Pre-Alpine valleys, the original characteristics and traditions of Gallic technique stubbornly survived, though the torques — that collar so typical of the northerners — became definitely a part of the Roman world, with its geometrical decorations far removed from classic taste. To these Italiot, Greek and Celtic influences, so very vital and indeed instrumental in establishing the pattern of Roman jewelry, we must add other elements which explain the widespread diffusion of objets d'art: fashion, the mainspring of so many habits; the general acceptance of exotic cults; and superstition, which was responsible for the amulets which the Romans wore. There was also the ostentation of the rich classes, which was certainly important in Roman society.

Examples illustrating these developments in Roman jewelry are not easy to find, particularly from the first centuries of the Empire. The organizers of the exhibition therefore searched the great archaeological centres of Italy in the hope of providing a rich and varied illustration of types and patterns rather than attempting to establish a chronological history which was bound to remain uncertain. In the field of *ornamenta muliebra* the best and most significant examples were selected; plain gold rings, rings set with stones, engagement and friendship rings, serpent-headed rings or rings decorated with the so-called Hercules-Knot, small *anuli* inscribed with good wishes, figures of friends, important men or images of the Junctio Destrarum. Also shown were adaptations of imperial gold coins — a fashion suggesting a decline in creative vision on the part of the craftsman, or perhaps even a way of amassing money. Certainly the owner of the Pompei oil-lamp (Plate 47) — its weight in gold is approximately 2 ½ lbs — could not have boasted about its aesthetic merits when he proudly showed it to his friends!

Roman matrons wore *armillae,* above or below the elbow. The most common type, allowing the artist's imagination free scope, seems to have been serpentine in shape (a shape that originated in foreign cults). There is no lack of similar armlets, consisting of a single tubular band in Western taste, or of more refined semi-spherical examples, apparently related to Celtic-Gallic culture.

In the necklaces collected at Pompei one is impressed by the lively colours of the inset stones contrasted against the warm background of the adornment. This can be seen in the splendid example in golden mail set with emeralds and oval stones of mother-of-pearl (Plate 49). But plain gold is often sufficient to create an object of rare beauty, as shown by the delightful necklace consisting of small ivy leaves, whose only decoration is the delicate veins of the leaves themselves.

Like their sisters from Greece, Roman women wore earrings, and old texts provide ample information about these *inaures* or *pendentes*. At times these seem to have been considered the height of ostentation. Seneca thundered against those women who, not content with one pearl (*iunio*) hanging from their ears, would group in a single pendant two or even three beautiful stones in order to set off the whiteness of the one against the alum colour of its neighbour. He wrote: " These extraordinary women probably believe that their husbands would not be tormented enough unless they wore two or three family fortunes (*patrimonia*) below each ear ". Writing on the subject of the ambitions of Roman women, Pliny mentioned that the stones suspended from their earrings were fitted so they would tinkle at the slightest movement of their heads; that is why this particular type of earring was called *crotalia*. Buckles (*fibulae*) were also much in use as personal adornments, and were often made of gold or set with precious stones and cameos (*fibulae gemmatae*).

The execution of these objects was entrusted to the capable hands of craftsmen many of whom have been recorded by historians because of their specialization. Among them were *celatores, aurifices, auratores inauratores, bratiari, margaritarii and anulari*.

As far as their techniques were concerned one should remember that pendants, earrings, necklaces and certain types of armlets were commonly obtained by casting.

For other products the goldsmith's basic elements were used, plates or threads of gold; the former were fashioned by hammering the bar, the latter by passing the molten metal through a threading-die over and over again, in ever decreasing quantities, to obtain thinner and thinner sections. Higher relief compositions were achieved by the *repoussé* method of hammering the metal from the reverse by means of stamped hammers (*spatulae*), or punches.

One fact is outstanding in all these objects: in the evolution of Roman jewelry, gold was at first the chief element in which the jewel was set. It constituted the setting and the frame of the precious stone. Gradually, however, the stone itself began to dominate, and it became more and more delicately bound to the gold. A new conception of the jewel was appearing, and was to develop even further during the Byzantine and Barbaric age.

ROMAN SILVER

The organizers of the Exhibition chose to show the silver products separately. This metal — because of the use of the lathe — is more directly connected with the representational arts. The lavish silver decorations of houses, furniture and table ware, with their engraved, sculptured or hammered figurations, make a considerable contribution to our knowledge of ancient paintings and sculptures. Often the themes and compositions admired on Roman silver repeat or echo Greek paintings and friezes which were thought to have disappeared for ever, and the rhythm of a god's or athlete's figure can enable one to identify an ancient and famous statuary model which has been lost. That is why — when examining the fine silver in plate from the so called House of Menander at Pompei — our attention is centred on the representational scenes which are the dominant element of these exceptional items.

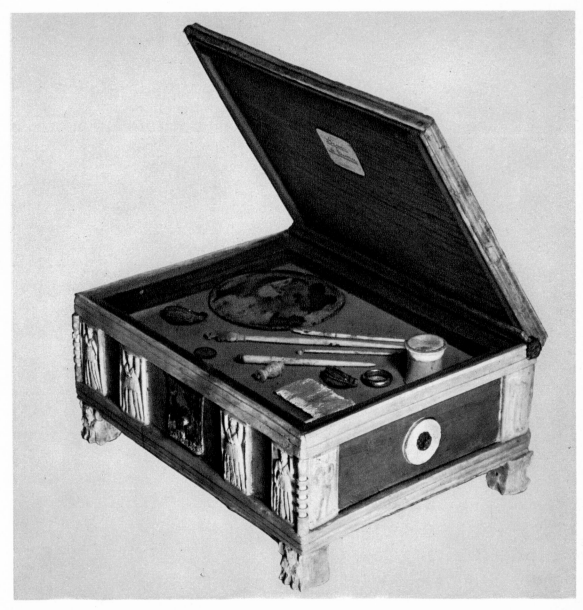

Cosmetic box of bone and metal, from Cuma - *Naples, Museo Archeologico Nazionale.*

Here, indeed, is living mythology, with centaurs and cupids recalling Hellenic scenes; a small Eros rides a bull (Plate 52 a) with a liveliness close to caricature and in strict rhythmical consistence with the original pictorial conceptions.

Some glasses and vases are decorated only with vegetable motifs; the most interesting is the one reproduced in Plate 52 b, with its beautifully fashioned leaves. In another silver vase, portraying a scene of Venus and Mars on its slope, one can see a decadent interpretation of the vegetable motif which, transformed as it is into vine-shoots, is developed academically for the purpose of filling in the spaces between the figures. Roman silverware was divided into two groups, and once again the guiding principle of selection was not so much chronology or typology, but rather the circumstances of the object's discovery. The first group comprises the " family silver ", exemplified by the proud possessions of a rich Pompeian household; the second is what can be described as the " hidden treasure ", that is to say a series of objects which were probably stored away during the troubled period when Italy — especially Northern Italy — was subject to transalpine invasions. Perhaps economic difficulties then made it advisable to remove any form of precious metal from circulation. This would explain why so many objects of various origins and ages were found across the countryside in Northern Italy near Alessandria (Marengo).

The bust of Emperor Lucios Verus (Plate 57) is the most important of these finds in that it also helps to define, with reasonable certainty, the chronology of other outstanding pieces. This is from the second century of the Roman Empire, that is to say the rule of the Antonine emperors; the character of Roman art can clearly be seen, although schemes and motifs stemming from the Greeks and readapted by the Romans to suit their own particular taste, are still present.

Many plastic works from all periods of Grecian art, created by both the noblest and humblest ancient masters, can be identified in the silver band with thirteen figures in high-relief found at Marengo (Plate 58). The splendid bell-shaped silver bowl (Plate 59) is another example of a simple decoration using vegetable motifs, although here it has lost the plastic naturality of the Pompeian vases and reveals more prominent draughtsmanship and decorative intention. This is also visible in the volutions and contours of the leaves and flowers on the " pulvinar " (Plate 59). The scene is completed and enlivened by the figure of a maenad drinking from a cup.

The Parabiago dish (Plate 65), with its vivid representational decoration, reveals that in the late Roman period creative drive gave way to repetitive schemes and to the Greek tradition based on Eastern inspiration. The dish is datable between the end of the 2nd and the beginning of the 3rd centuries A. D., when themes from Syria and Asia Minor appeared within the Empire (then ruled by the Severus family.

The Cesena missorium (Plate 67) is more difficult to date. This masterpiece was perhaps executed by a Byzantine engraver who settled near Ravenna. The scenic composition depicted on the bottom of the plate recalls the Asian and African late-

Apulian vase decorated with a Gynaeceum scene - *Taranto, Museo Nazionale.*

antique period, but the thorough treatment of the figures and details reminds one of miniatures of the 5th century A. D., illustrating the Iliad and the Aeneid, and still to be seen in the Vatican and Ambrosiana libraries. On the other hand, the blending and contrasts of tints in the latter works have been replaced in the Cesena missorium by a new polychromy obtained by blending together gold, silver and niello (a black

Fragment of silver depicting a religious scene - *Bologna, Museo Civico.*

composition consisting of metallic alloys, used for filling in engraved designs on silver or other metals).

The last item in the silver section of the exhibition is the small *capsella* (reliquary) from Grado (Plate 66), with figurations that are already typically Christian and bear no relationship to traditional classic conceptions.

BARBARIC JEWELRY

The political, social and economic crisis of the Roman Empire brought about a momentous transformation in the marketing and diffusion of jewelry. The tendency to hoard, caused by inflation and devaluation of currency, gave the jewel a new significance. From a simple adornment it became a commodity of exchange. This is why the jewels produced at this time were bigger, with more gold and precious stones, and were intended for people who, in a society already affected by barbaric elements, could impress only by the richness of their attire.

This historical period is reflected, for example, in the rings (Plate 61) and bracelets which are part of the treasure of the Royal Theatre at Parma, or in the collection found in the burial grounds of Zeccone (Pavia). Each piece of jewelry reveals poverty of imagination but also prosperity and opulence; the insertion of coins into necklace pendants (Plate 60) stresses even further the economic function of the jewel.

The mixture of Roman traditional and barbaric forms is fairly obvious in the fibulae fashioned in the shape of Latin crosses. It is even more obvious in the linear decoration and in the particular contrast of lights between the luminous foreground and the shaded background of the fretwork (*opus interassile*) peculiar to the Byzantine jewel. To this period belong the Otranto earrings (Plate 68 a), the Palermo necklace and, to a lesser degree, the Syracuse ring (Plate 70). Further progress is shown by the Senise collection with its magnificent earrings (Plate 77 b) in which the chromatic decoration of plastic figures is strongly suggestive of mosaic technique.

The vast and tumultuous migrations from Western and Central Europe into Italy following the end of the Western Empire caused considerable changes in living habits. As a result the function of jewelry in social life became increasingly important; elegance and ostentation were now principal requirements of social success. New schemes and motifs for jewelry were introduced from Southern Russia and Northern Europe which, coming into contact with classic tradition, degenerated into decorational mannerism. Yet products commonly known as Gothic were a blend of classic and East-European themes. A good example of this is the Desana treasure, with its great fibulae decorated with leaves and enriched with gems and enamel, and its beautiful jewels, such as the filigree diadem of amethyst, emeralds and garnets.

The Lombards, who overran Italy after the Goths (approximately 568 A. D.), introduced the entwined band into jewelry, but under their rule the traditional forms continued to be used. Typical of this period are large fibulae with semicircular or rectangular heads, with small wreath-shaped discs which gradually evolved into the schematic form of a bird; necklaces decorated with imperial gold coins, and splendid laminae decorated with low-reliefs and used as covers for leather bridles and reins. Equally numerous are the large discs (Plates 71 a and b) with a figure or a stone in the centre, surrounded by spiralled filigreed motifs.

The *cloisonné* technique first appeared at this time, a technique in which thin gold plates are set on edge on a foundation plaque and precious stones or enamels are then set into them. Often this type of decoration is in the shape of a cross. But small crosses of gold laminae with arms of equal length (Plates 74 and 81) are proof that the Lombards had absorbed the Christian faith and were even propagating it by means of their jewelry. Now on the threshold of the 7th century, the evolution of ancient Italian jewelry had more or less come full circle. The horizon already was in sight, gleaming with aspirations and hopes which were to become the new artistic vision of medieval civilization.

Silver Cross - *Ravenna, Museo Arcivescovile.*

Solid gold statuette of a wild goat, Greco-Persian - *Naples, Museo Archeologico Nazionale.*

If we examine works by ancient jewelers with a magnifying glass or under a microscope, we have difficulty in deciding just where technique ends and art begins, these two elements being so closely interconnected.
For this reason it is important to know a little more about the technical details mentioned in the introduction and following chapters of this book. From the ancient Etruscan period to this day not only the technique of execution of jewelry, but even the main tools of the trade, have changed little.

Hammered work. This is derived from the oldest method of treating gold, and consists of hammering the metal first into threads and laminae (thin layers of the metal) and then in " hammering out " the lamina from the reverse side. The treatment of the figurative or geometrical elements was executed later as part of the finishing. The same technique was applied to stamping, a process which clearly means the mechanical repetition of a subject.
The study of how gold was welded in ancient times has fascinated technicians and scientists throughout the centuries because of the known difficulty of heating the metal up to the necessary temperature for fusion (1063 degrees Centigrade). Pliny mentions a system which included the addition — with a thread and a nail of gold used as a means of soldering — of a certain quantity of silver. The amalgam thus obtained allowed fusion at a lower temperature. Silver itself was often used with the addition of resins; the Romans used lead for the same purposes. Present day jewelers use borax and it is not improbable that this substance was part of the " Krisocolla " mentioned by Pliny.

Filigree. At first the laminae were delicately hammered into wire, but later proper threading-dies were used with increasingly thinner sections; then a background of gold wire was laid down, creating a delicate effect of arabesques that can still be admired in jewelry today.

Granulation. Ancient Etruscan jewelers were perhaps reluctant to reveal the secrets of their technique; that is why modern experts are still puzzled by the methods they must have used to ensure that the tiny globules of gold dust adhered to the smooth metal surface. There are various theories about this: that the molten metal was made to pass through an extremely fine sieve, or that the golden wire was melted until it became possible to transform it into small particles, which could be picked up and made even finer by rolling them between two plates of metal or glass. A third, and more acceptable theory, based on experiments made in Valencia, is that gold dust, mixed with adhesive borax, was scattered upon the red-hot metal bar or plate.

British technicians have developed a system similar to autogenous welding whereby the foundation metal and the globules of gold dust are heated almost to fusion point; the welding is then effected by means of a copper hydrate and adhesive substance. Most recent experiments have revealed in early jewelry the presence of amber apparently used with the same function as a resin in welding.

Opus interassile (fretwork). This technique originated in Syria. The line is carved deeply with a burin and the superfluous parts are hammered or chiselled away, after which any remaining irregularity is smoothed out.

Gem stones. The insertion of precious stones into jewelry imposed new procedures. At first the stones were attached to the necklaces or pendants by means of gold threads; later they were inserted into the metal which had previously been cut expressly so that its carved mounts would hold the stone firmly in place. Cast gold threads were added to strengthen the setting.

Enamels. These are pieces of coloured glass obtained by the fusion of glass fragments or powdered glass. They were inserted into filigreed jewels or welded upon the background with cast gold threads.

ABBREVIATIONS

Reviews and Periodicals

Acta A.	*Acta Archaeologica* - Copenhagen.
Ann. Inst.	*Annali dell'Istituto di Corrispondenza Archeologica* - Rome.
Ant. Denk.	*Antike Denkmäler*, IV - Berlin, 1929.
Arch. Class.	*Archeologia Classica* - Rome, 1949, ff.
Atti Acc. S. L. P.	*Atti della Reale Accademia di Scienze, Lettere ed Arti* - Palermo.
Atti I. V. S.	*Atti dell'Istituto Veneto di Scienze, Lettere ed Arti* - Venice, 1956, p. 55.
Atti Mem. P. Rom.	*Atti e Memorie della R. Deputazione di Storia Patria della Provincia di Romagna* - Bologna.
Att. Soc. Piem. Arch.	*Atti della Società Piemontese di Antichità e Belle Arti* - Turin.
Boll. Stor. Bibl. Sub.	*Bollettino Storico Bibliografico Subalpino* - Turin.
Boll. St. Pavese	*Bollettino Storico Pavese*, II - 1894.
Bull. Inst.	*Bollettino dell'Istituto di Corrispondenza Archeologica* - Rome, 1875 ff.
F. A.	*Fasti Archeologici, Bollettino Annuale di Archeologica Classica* - Florence, 1946, ff.
Historia	*Historia, Zeitschrift für Alte Geschichte Verlag für Kunst und Wissenschaft* - Baden-Baden, Wiesbaden, 1950 ff.
Ill. Lon. News	*Illustrated London News* - London.
Mem. Am. Ac.	*Memories of the American Academy in Rome* - Rome-New York.
Mon. Ant.	*Monumenti di Antichità pubblicati a cura dell'Accademia dei Lincei* - Milan.
Mon. Inst.	*Monumenti dell'Istituto di Corrispondenza Archeologica* - Rome & Paris, 1829-1891.
MZK	*Mitteilungen der K. K. Central Commission zur Erforschung und Erhaltung der Kunst und Historischen Denkmäler* - Vienna, 1875 ff.
Not. Sc.	*Notizie Scavi di Antichità, Accademia Nazionale dei Lincei* - Rome, 1876 ff.
Rend. Acc. Napoli	*Rendiconti Accademia Archeologica di Lettere e Belle Arti di Napoli.*
Rend. Linc.	*Rendiconti della Accademia Nazionale dei Lincei* - Rome.
Röm. Mitt.	*Mitteilungen des Deutschen Archäologischen Instituts, Römische Abteilung* - Rome.

Sibrium	*Sibrium; Centro di Studi Preistorici e Archeologici -* Varese.
St. M.	*Studi e Materiali di Archeologia e di Numismatica -* Florence.
S. T.	*Zeitschrift für Ethnologie.*
Z. f. E.	*Studi Trentini di Scienze Storiche* - Trento.

Books and articles

Aberg, Goten	N. Aberg, *Die Goten und Langobarden in Italien* - Uppsala, 1923.
Anti, Museo di Venezia	C. Anti, *Museo Archeologico del Palazzo Reale di Venezia* - Rome, 1930.
Aurigemma, Museo di Spina	S. Aurigemma, *Il R. Museo di Spina in Ferrara* - Ferrara, 1936.
Brozzi-Tagliaferri, Arte Longobarda, I	M. Brozzi - A. Tagliaferri, *Arte Longobarda*: I, *La scultura figurativa su marmo* - Cividale, 1950.
Brusin, Scavi	G. Brusin, *Gli Scavi di Aquielia*, 1934.
Dall'Osso, Guida	I. Dall'Osso, *Guida illustrata del Museo Nazionale di Ancona* - Ancona, 1915.
De Lama	P. De Lama, *Memorie intorno ad alcuni preziosi ornamenti antichi d'oro scoperti a Parma nell'anno 1821* - Rome, 1824.
Ducati, Guida	P. Ducati, *Guida del Museo Civico di Bologna* - Bologna, 1923.
Ducati, A. E.	P. Ducati, *Storia dell'Arte etrusca* - Florence, 1927.
Ducati, Bologna	P. Ducati, *Bologna, I tempi antichi, Storia di Bologna,* I - Bologna, 1928.
Ebers, Antichità Sarde	Ebers, « Antichità Sarde e loro provenienza », in *Ann. dell'Istituto* - Rome, 1883.
Etruria Padana	*Mostra dell'Etruria Padana e della Città di Spina* - Bologna, 1960.
Falchi, Vetulonia	I. Falchi, *Vetulonia e la sua necropoli antichissima* - Florence, 1891.
Forlati Tamaro, Itinerario	B. Forlati Tamaro, *Itinerario del Museo Archeologico di Venezia* - Rome, 1950.
Fuchs, Langobard. Goldblattkreuze	S. Fuchs, *Die langobardischen Goldblattkreuze aus der Zone südwärts der Alpen* - Berlin, 1938.
Gervasio, Bronzi Antichi	A. Gervasio, *Bronzi antichi e ceramica geometrica del Museo di Bari* - Bari, 1921.
Giglioli, A. E.	G. Q. Giglioli, *L'arte etrusca* - Milan, 1936.
Grenier, Bologne	Grenier, *Bologne villanovienne et étrusque,* 1912.
Helbig, Führer	W. Helbig, *Führer durch die öffentlichen Sammlungen klassischer Altertümer in Rom,* I, II, 1912-1913.

XXVIII

Inghirami, Mon. Etr.	Inghirami, *Monumenti Etruschi o di etrusco nome ecc.*, 1821, 1826.
Jenny-Volbach, Germanischer Schmuck	W. von Jenny - W. Volbach, *Germanischer Schmuck des frühen Mittelalters* - Berlin, 1933.
Johnstone, St. Etr., 1932	M. A. Johnstone « The Etruscan Collection in the Public Museum at Liverpool », in *Studi Etruschi*, VI, pp. 448, 452.
Marconi, Itinerario	P. Marconi, *Itinerario R. Museo Nazionale di Palermo, Sezione Archeologica* - Rome, 1932.
Mayer, Apulien	A. Mayer, *Apulien vor und während der Hellenisierung* - Leipzig - Berlin, 1914.
Mengarelli, Castel Trosimo	R. Mengarelli « La necropoli barbarica di Castel Trosino », in *Monumenti Antichi dei Lincei*, XII, 1902.
Milano, RMA	L. A. Milani, *Il R. Museo Archeologico di Firenze*, 1912.
Minto, Populonia	A. Minto, *Populonia* - Florence, 1943.
Monaco, Museo Antichità	G. Monaco, *Il R. Museo di Antichità di Parma* - Rome, 1943.
Montelius	O. Montelius, *La civilisation primitive en Italie depuis l'introduction des métaux*, II, 190, 1905.
Mostra Etrusca	*Catalogo Mostra dell'Arte e della Civiltà Etrusca* - Milan, 1955.
Mostra Scult. Etrusca	*Catalogo Mostra della Scultura Etrusca* - Florence, 1952.
Mühlestein	H. Mühlestein, *Die Kunst der Etrusker* - Berlin, 1929.
Muller, Phöniz. Kunstgew.	V. Müller, « Das Phönizische Kunstgewerbe », in *Geschichte des Kunstgewerbes*, IV - Berlin, 1930.
Ori Emilia	*Ori e Argenti dell'Emilia Antica* - Bologna, 1958.
Orsi, Sicilia Bizantina	P. Orsi, *Sicilia Bizantina* - Rome, 1942.
Pace, Sicilia antica	B. Pace, *Arte e Civiltà della Sicilia Antica* - Rome, 1935-1940.
Panazza, Civici Musei	G. Panazza, *I civici Musei e la Pinacoteca di Brescia* - Bergamo, 1958.
Pasqui-Paribeni, Nocera Umbra	A. Pasqui - R. Paribeni, « Necropoli barbarica di Nocera Umbra », in *Mon. Ant.*, XXV, 1918.
Perrot-Chipiez	G. Perrot - C. Chipiez, *Histoire de l'Art dans l'Antiquité*, I-X, 1882, 1914.
Pinza, Materiali per l'etnologia	G. Pinza, *Materiali per la Etnologia antica toscano-laziale* - Milan, 1914.
Riccioni, Sepolcreto Aureli	G. Riccioni, « Il sepolcreto felsineo Aureli », in *Studi Etruschi*, XXII, 1952-1953, pp. 233, 285.
Rizzini, Catalogo dei Bronzi	P. Rizzini, *Il Museo di Brescia, Catalogo dei Bronzi.*
Rizzini, Civici Musei	P. Rizzini, *Illustrazione dei Civici Musei di Brescia*, 1911.
Rizzini, Oggetti Barbarici; Supplemento	P. Rizzini, *Gli oggetti barbarici raccolti nel Museo di Brescia*, ivi, 1894; *Supplemento agli oggetti barbarici* - Brescia, 1914.
Rosemberg	M. Rosemberg, *Granulation*, I, 1915; II, 1916; III, 1917.

Schaffran E. *Schaffran, Die Kunst der Langobarden in Italien* - Jena, 1941.

Siviero R. Siviero, *Gli ori e le ambre del Museo Nazionale di Napoli* - Florence, 1954.

Taramelli, Museo di Cagliari A. Taramelli, *Guida del Museo Nazionale di Cagliari* - Cagliari, 1914.

Venturi A. Venturi, *Storia dell'Arte Italiana*, II - Milan, 1902.

Werner, Langobard, Fibeln J. Werner - B. Bischoff, « Langobardische Grabfunde aus Reggio Emilia », in *Germania*, 1952.

Werner, Langobard, Fibeln J. Werner, *Die langobardischen Fibeln aus Italien* - Berlin, 1950.

Werner, Imola J. Werner, « Die Schwerter von Imola ecc. », in *Acta Archaeologica*, XXI, 1950.

BIBLIOGRAPHY

Daremberg - Saglio - Pottier, *Dictionnaire des antiquités*: " Anulus, Armilla, Aurilex, Aurum; Bulla; Brattea; Caelatura; Electrum, Fibula; Gemma; Inaures ".

Enciclopedia dell'Arte classica e orientale: " Ambra; Bracciale; Collana ".

M. Eber, Reallexikon der Vorgeschichte, Berlin: " Gold; Goldfunde; Goldschmiedekunst; Granulation ".

F. H. Marshall, " Ringe ", in Pauly-Wissowa, *Real Encyclopaedie,* cc. 808-833.

Ch. De Linas, *Les origines de l'orfèvrerie cloisonnée,* Paris, 1877.

C. ed E. Calandra, " Necropoli Barbarica scoperta a Testona ", in *Atti Società Belle Arti prov.* Turin, IV, 1880.

H. Blümner, *Technologie und Terminologie der Gewerbe und Künste bei Griechen und Römern,* IV Leipzig, 1886.

A. Héron de Villfosse, " Le trésor de Boscoreale ", in *Monumenti Piot,* V, Paris, 1899.

A. Furtwängler, *Die antiken Gemmen,* 3 vols. Leipzig-Berlin, 1900.

E. Pernice - C. Winter, *Der Hildesheimer Silberfund,* 1901.

R. Mengarelli, " La necropoli barbarica di Castel Trosino ", in *Monumenti Antichi dei Lincei,* XII, 1902, cc. 236 (Mengarelli, *Mon. Ant.,* XII).

K. Hadaczek, *Der Ohrschmuck der Griechen und Etrusker,* Vienna, 1903.

F. Zimmermann, " Les foyers de production de l'or dans l'antiquité et dans le moyen âge ", in *Bulletin de la Société géographique de Lyon,* XX, 1905.

F. H. Marshall, *Catalogue of the Jewellery in the British Museum,* London, 1911.

O. Rubenshon, *Hellenistisches Silbergerät in antiken Gibsabgüssern,* Berlin, 1911.

E. Babelon, *Le trésor d'argenterie de Berthouville,* Paris, 1916.

R. Paribeni, " Necropoli barbarica di Nocera Umbra ", in *Monumenti Antichi dei Lincei,* XXV, 1918, cc 137-352 (Paribeni, *Mon. Ant.,* XXV).

A. Minto, *Marsigliana d'Albegna,* Florence, 1921.

N. Aberg, *Die Goten und Langobarden in Italien,* Uppsala, 1923.

A. De Ridder, *Catalogue sommaire des bijoux antiques des Musées du Louvre,* Paris, 1924.

G. Moreti, " Oreficeria del Museo di Ancona e la civiltà picena del periodo gallico ", in *Dedalo,* V, 1924, pp. 3, 17.

D. Randall - M. A. Mac Iver, *Villanovians and Early Etruscans,* Oxford, 1924.

C. S. Blinkenberg, *Fibules grecques et orientales,* Copenhagen, 1926.

R. Zahn, "Hellenistischer Goldschmuck und der Goldkranz von Armento ", in *Antike Denkmäler,* IV, Berlin, 1929.

Geschichte des Kunstgewerbes, IV, Berlin, 1930; V. Müller, "Das Phönizische Kunstgewerbe ", pp. 142-156; F. Matz, " Das Kunstgewerbe Altitaliens", pp. 183-249; Id., " Das Kunstgewerbe der römischen Kaiserzeit ", pp. 317-321, 340-344.

P. Demargne, " Bijoux minoens de Mallia ", in *Bull. Cor. Hell.*, LIV, 1930, p. 404-421.

P. Wuilleumier, *Le trésor de Tarente*, Paris, 1930, (pp. 73-75).

A. Maiuri, *La casa del Menandro e il suo tesoro di argenteria*, Rome, 1932.

R. Bartoccini, " La tomba degli Ori di Canosa ", in *Japigia*, VI, 1935, pp. 225-226.

P. Jacobsthal, " Early Celtic Art ", in *The Burlington Magazine*, LXII, 1935, pp. 113-127, pls. I-III.

B. Salin, *Die Altgermanische Tierornamentik*, Stockholm, 1935.

A. Levi, " La patera argentea di Parabiago ", in *Opere d'arte dell'Istituto di Archeologia e Storia dell'Arte*, V.

G. Bendinelli, " Il Tesoro di argenteria di Marengo ", in *Monumenti d'Arte Antica, a cura della R. Accademia delle Scienze di Torino*, Turin, 1937, I.

A. Ippei, "Guss und Treibarbeit in Silber", in *97 Bw. Pr.*, Berlin-Leipzig, 1937.

S. Fuchs, *Die Langobardischen Goldblattreuze aus der Zone südwarts der Alpen*, Berlin, 1938.

A. Adriani, " Le gobelet en argent des amours vendangeurs des Musées d'Alexandrie ", in *Société royale d'Archéologie d'Alexandrie*, I, 1939.

L. Breglia, " Le oreficerie del Museo di Taranto ", in *Japigia*, X; 1939, pp. 5-54.

Ch. Alexander, *The Metropolitan Museum of Art, Greek and Etruscan Jewellery*, a picture-book, New York, 1940.

G. M. A. Richter, *Handbook of the Etruscan Collection in the Metropolitan Museum of Art*, New York, 1937.

L. Breglia, *Catalogo delle Oreficerie del Museo Nazionale di Napoli*, Rome, 1941.

R. Hautzsch, " Die Langobardische Schmuckkunst in Oberitalien", in *Römisches Jahrbuch für Kunstgeschichte*, V, 1941, pp. 1-48.

E. Schaffran, *Die Kunst der Langobarden in Italien*, Jena, 1941.

H. Quiring, " Das Gold im Altertum ", in *Forschungen und Fortschritte*, 1942, p. 55 ff.

V. Viale " Recenti ritrovamenti archeologici a Vercelli e nel Vercellese. Il Tesoro di Desana ", in *Bollettino storico bibliografico subalpino*, XLIV, 1942, pp. 1-23.

C. Cecchelli, *I monumenti del Friuli*, Cividale-Roma, 1943.

B. Segall, " Some Sources of Early Greek Jewelry ", in *Bulletin of the Museum of Fine Arts*, Boston, XLI, 1943, p. 42-46.

E. Sundwall, *Die älteren italischen Fibeln*, Berlin, 1943.

P. Jacobsthal, *Early Celtic Art*, Oxford, 1944.

P. Cintas, *Amulettes puniques*, Paris, 1946.

P. E. Arias, " Il piatto argenteo di Cesena ", in *Annuario della Scuola Archeologica di Atene*, XXIV-XXVI, *Not. Sc.* VIII-X, 1946-1948, p. 309 ff.

A. Andrén, " Oreficeria e plastica etrusche ", in *Opuscula Archaeologica*, Lund, 1948, V, pp. 91-112.

J. Werner, *Die Langobardischen Fibeln aus Italien*, Berlin, 1950.

C. Albizzati - A. Stenico, " Osservazioni su oggetti del VII secolo a. C. trovati nell'Italia centrale ", in *Acme*, V, 1952, pp. 589-606.

J. Werner - B. Bischoff, " Langobardische Grabfunde aus Reggio Emilia ", in *Germania,* 30, 1952, fasc. 2.

P. Amandry, *Collection H. Stathatos, Bijoux antiques,* Strasbourg, 1953.

H. Battke, *Geschichte des Ringes,* Baden-Baden, 1953.

G. Maggi, " La terminologia dell'oro nel greco e nel latino ", in *Rendiconti Accademia Archeologica Lettere e Belle Arti di Napoli,* XX, VII, 1953, pp. 249-277.

A. Riegi, *Industria artistica tardo-romana,* B. Forlati Tamaro and M. T. Ronga Leoni, Florence, 1953.

J. Haekin, " Nouvelles recherches archéologiques à Bégram ", in *Mémoires de la Délégation Archéologique Française en Afghanistan,* XI, Paris, 1954.

R. Siviero, *Gli ori e le ambre del Museo Nazionale di Napoli,* Florence, 1954.

C. Singer - E. J. Holmayard - A. R. Hall, *History of Technology,* I, Oxford, 1954.

G. Becatti, *Oreficerie antiche dalle minoiche alle barbariche,* Rome, 1955.

E. Coche de la Ferté, *Les Bijoux antiques,* Paris, 1956.

A. Adriani, " Divagazioni intorno ad una coppa paesistica del Museo di Alessandria ", in *Documenti e Ricerche di Arte Alessandria,* III-IV, Rome 1959.

G. Pesce, *Sardegna punica,* Cagliari, 1960.

M. Degani, *Il Tesoro romano barbarico di Reggio Emilia* (in preparation).

PLATES

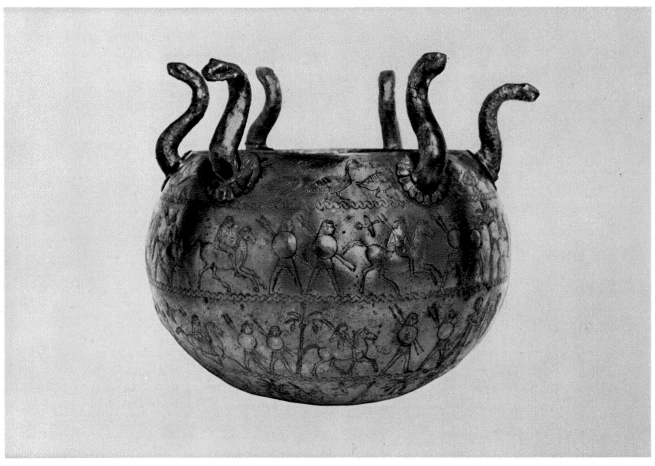

Plate 2

PLATE 2 - Small silver basin coated with gold. Decorated with lightly hammered-out figures divided into four bands, and representing pastoral and rural scenes alternating with duels and lion hunts. Palms and birds fill up the empty spaces and separate the groups of figures. A lion — symbolizing the king — claws at a defeated enemy in the lower band. The six snakes were welded on to the upper band sometime after the original execution. 7th century B. C. Height 5 1/2 ins; diameter 5 7/8 ins.

ROME, Museo Villa Giulia. — FROM PALESTRINA, Bernardini Tomb. — Bibliography: Helbig, *Führer*, n. 1585; Curtis, *Mem. Am. Ac.*, III, 1919, n. 23, pl. XII; Mühlestein, fig. 16, 19; Giglioli, *A. E.*, p. 33, 1; Becatti, n. 219; *Mostra Etrusca*, Milan, n. 94, Cologne, n. 20.

PLATE 3 - Large gold clasp, worn by an Etruscan chieftain on shoulder or chest. The vivid decoration consists of stamped figures of chimaerae, crouching lions, harpies and human beings and is further enriched with granulated details. This is the most outstanding example of the high technical standards of the Etruscan jewelers, who were obviously influenced by Eastern taste at this, the earliest phase of their production. 7th century B. C. Length 6 3/4 ins; width 2 5/8 ins.

ROME, Museo Villa Giulia. — FROM PALESTRINA, Bernardini Tomb. — Bibliography: Helbig, *Führer*, n. 1577; Pinza, *Materiali per l'etnologia*, pl. XVII; Montelius, pl. CCCLXX, 7; Curtis, *Mem. Am. Ac.*, III, 1919, pl. I, 1 & 2, pl. II, 1 & 2; Ducati, *A. E.*, p. 136, fig. 137; Giglioli, *A. E.*, pl. XXVa; *Mostra Etrusca*, Milan, n. 14. Cologne, n. 18; Becatti pl. A.

2

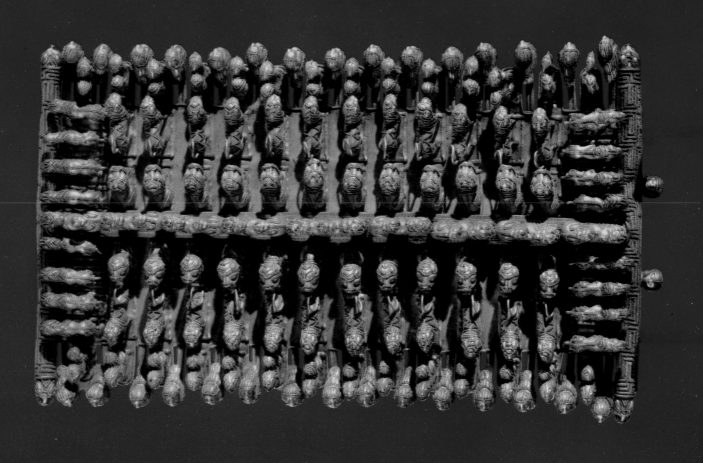

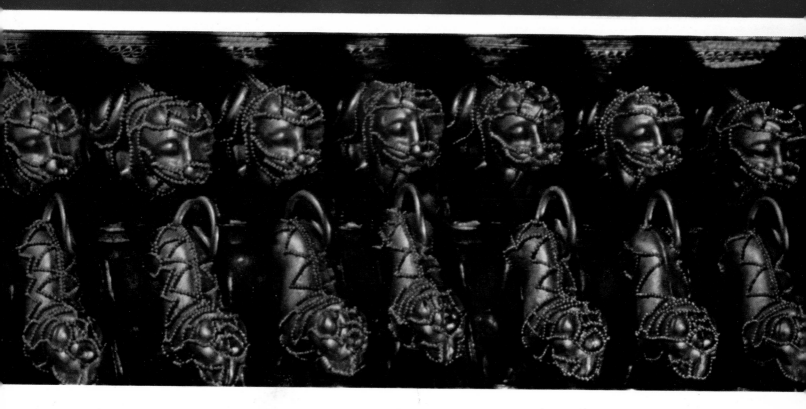

PLATE 4 a - Gold drinking cup of simple and elegant form. Its surface is as smooth as polished glass. The two pairs of Sphinxes above the handles were executed by means of hammering and granulation. 7th century B. C. Height 3 ¹/₈ ins; diameter 3 ¹/₂ ins.

ROME, Museo Villa Giulia. — FROM PALESTRINA, Bernardini Tomb. — Bibliography: Mon. Inst., X, pl. XXI; Bull. d'Inst., 1876, p. 125; Helbig, *Führer*, n. 1584; Curtis, *Mem. Am. Ac.*, III, 1919, n. 20, pl. X; *Mostra Etrusca*, Milan, n. 95, Cologne, n. 21; Becatti, n. 235, pl. XLVI.

PLATE 4 b - Cylinder of laminated gold, once the central part of a clasp decorated with figures. Its granulated decorations of a geometrical design are divided into three bands. 7th century B. C. Length 7 ¹/₂ ins; diameter ³/₈ in.

ROME, Museo Villa Giulia. — FROM PALESTRINA, Bernardini Tomb. — Bibliography: Helbig, *Führer*, n. 1580 (5 & 6). *Mem. Am. Ac.*, III, 1919, p. 25, pl. IV, V; Giglioli, *A. E.* pl. XXV c.

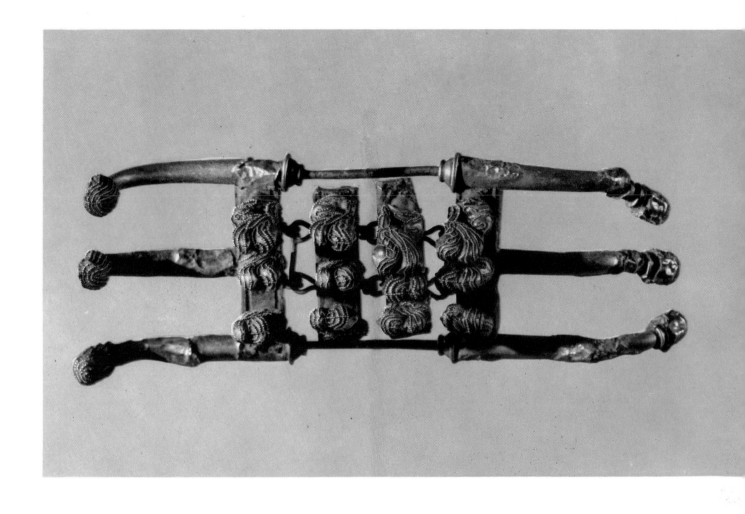

PLATE 5 - Gold clasp consisting of two parts held together by a number of hooks at the centre. Each element is composed of three small cylinders bent outwards and inwards, with human heads at the outer ends. The central part of the clasp is decorated with hammered and granulated figures of sphinxes. 7th century B. C. Length 3 ³/₈ ins; width 1 in.

ROME, Museo Villa Giulia. — FROM PALESTRINA, Bernardini Tomb. — Bibliography: Curtis, *Mem. Ac.*, III. 1919, p. 29, pl. IX.

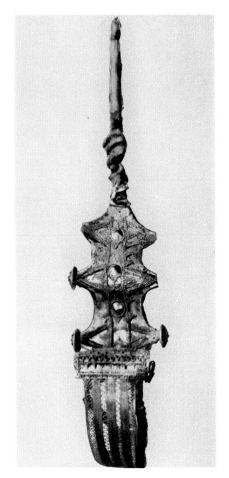

Plate 6 a   Plate 6 b

PLATE 6 a - Large pin with a gold sphere decorated with small discs and palm-leaves and surmounted by a bird. A filigreed work. 7th century B. C. Length 3 ¹/₂ ins.

> MILAN, Museo Poldi-Pezzoli (inventory no. 602).

PLATE 6 b - This fibula in the shape of a tortuous arch, in silver lamina plated with gold, comes from Marsiliana. The filigreed decoration of one part of the arc contrasts with the granulation of the arched sector. Second half of 7th century B. C. Length 4 ³/₄ ins.

> FLORENCE, Museo Archeologico (inventory no. 92170). — FROM MARSILIANA, Circolo di Perazzeta. — Bibliography: Minto, *Marsiliana*, p. 161, pl. XIII, 4; Sundwall, 248, n. 3.

PLATE 7 - These two gold armlets, found in a burial ground at Vetulonia, seem extraordinarily modern in design. The two filigreed bands forming the main body of the jewel on the right are decorated at one end with hammered female faces. Second half of 7th century B. C. Length 8 ins; height 1 ³/₈ ins; diameter 2 ³/₈ ins.

> FLORENCE, Museo Archeologico (inventory no. 75511-75512). — FROM VETULONIA, Tumulo delle Miglia-rine. — Bibliography: Falchi, *Not. Sc.*, 1894, p. 342; Karo, *ST. M., II*, p. 106, fig. 60; Montelius, II, c. 914, pl. CCIII, 3; Mac Iver p. 147, pl. XXVIII, 6; Mühlestein, fig. 85 b; Giglioli, *A. E.*, pl. XXI, 3; *Mostra Scult. Etr.*, n. 27; Albizzati-Stenico, *Acme*, V, 3, 1952, pp. 597-598; *Mostra Etrusca*, n. 110, 111; Becatti, n. 263, pl. LXVI.

Plate 7

PLATE 8 - This fibula in the shape of a rigid arc comes also from *Vetulonia*. Its body consists of a winged sphinx made out of two laminae hammered together. The band below depicts a granulated frieze of running animals. Second half of 7th century B. C. Length 3 ³/₈ ins.

FLORENCE, Museo Archeologico (inventory no. 77262). — FROM VETULONIA, Tomba del Littore. — Bibliography: Falchi, *Not. Sc.*, 1898, p. 151, fig. 13; Karo, *ST. M. I.*, p. 255, fig. 25, pl. IV, 7; Montelius, II, col. 879, pl. CXCIII, 2; Mac Iver, 146, pl. XXVIII, 1; Giglioli, *A. E.*, pl. XX, 12; *Mostra Scult. Etr.*, n. 24 *Mostra Etrusca*, n. 108; Becatti, n. 252 a-b, pl. LX, 262 a-b; Benedetti, *St. Etr.*, XXVII, p. 246, n. 45, pls. XX, c, & XXVIII, p. 467 ff.

PLATE 9 a - These two discs of thin laminated gold were part of a necklace of yellow amber beads alternating with bullae (ornaments used as protection against the evil eye). The decorations of the discs, in light relief, portray meanders, spirals and stylized wolf-fangs. 7th century B. C. Diameter of discs 2 ³/₈ ins.

ROME, Museo Villa Giulia. — FROM BISENZIO, Necropoli dell'Olmo Bello. — Bibliography: Paribeni, *Not Sc.*, 1928, p. 437, fig. 5.

PLATE 9 b - This gold fibula comes from the Lictor's Tomb at Vetulonia. Its form is traditional, of the typical " leech " type. The simplicity of the piece could be considered as an early reaction to the baroque appearance of other jewels, overladen with decorations in the Eastern style. Granulated figures of animals, both real and imaginary, are visible on this object. Second half of 7th century B. C. Length 5 ⁷/₈ ins.

FLORENCE, Museo Archeologico (inventory no. 77261). — Bibliography: Falchi, *Not. Sc.*, 1898, p. 151, fig. 14-16; Karo, *ST. M., I*, p. 258-259, fig. 27-28, pl. IV, 9 & 10; Rosemberg, *Granulation*, p. 58, fig. 91; Becatti, n. 253, a, b, pl. LX; Benedetti, *St. Etr.*, XXVII, p. 245, n. 44, pls. XX & XXVIII, p. 467 ff.

Plate 8

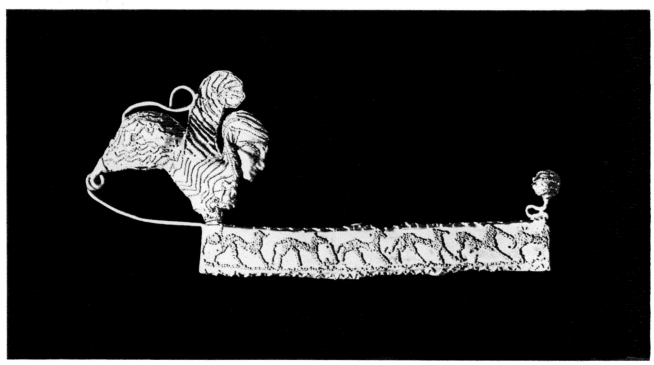

Plate 9 a

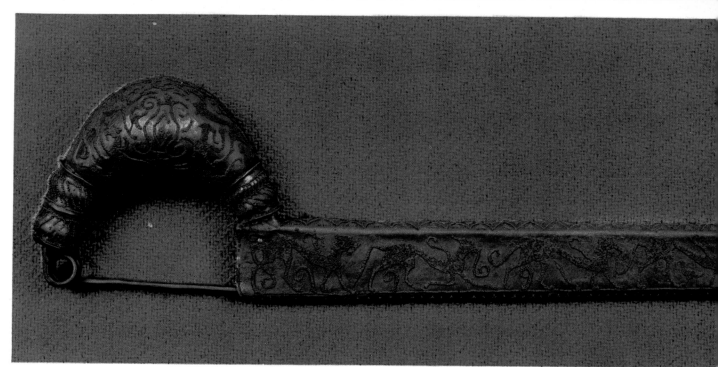

Plate 9 b

9

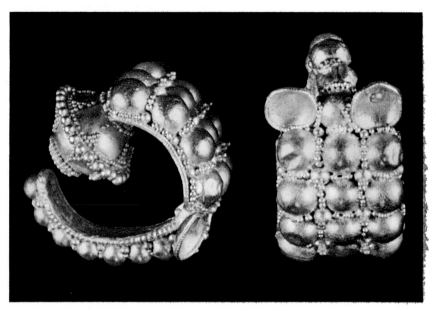

PLATE 10 - These two tapered earrings are decorated with small globes held together by a network of small pearls. The larger extremity of each jewel is composed of a sphere surrounded by a crown of small pearls. 5th century B. C. Diameter 1 in.

BOLOGNA, Museo Civico. — FROM BOLOGNA, Sepolcreto della Certosa, Tomb no. 86. — Bibliography: Zannoni, pl. XLIII, n. 12, p. 170; Montelius, pl. CII, fig. 10; Ducati, *Bologna*, p. 265, fig. 122; Id., *A. E.*, p. 331, fig. 378; *Ori Emilia*, n. 28-29, fig. 4.

PLATE 11 a - Circular bract of laminated gold. At the centre, bordered by a stylized sheaf of corn, a profile of the god Apollo shows the influence of Sicilian coins of the early 5th century B. C. Diameter 1 in.

FLORENCE, Museo Archeologico (inventory no. 81100). — FROM VETULONIA, acquired by Lancetti in 1903. — Bibliography: *Mostra Scult. Etr.*, n. 116; *Mostra Etrusca*, n. 132-133.

PLATE 11 b - Gold clasp consisting of four acorns. Each acorn is decorated with granulation in the upper part and filigree in the lower part. End 7th - beginning 6th centuries B. C. Length 1 ³/₈ ins.

FLORENCE, Museo Archeologico (inventory no. 92177). — FROM POPULONIA. — Bibliography: Minto, *Not. Sc.*, 1940, p. 378, fig. 3, 7; Id., *Populonia*, p. 138, pl. XXVIII, 7; *Mostra Scult. Etr.*, n. 28; *Mostra Etrusca*, n. 116.

Plate 11 a

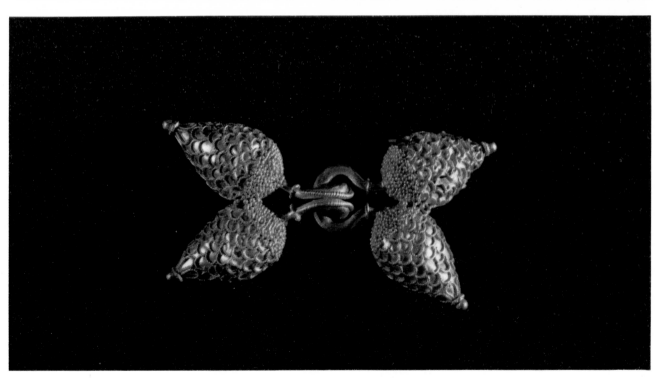

Plate 11 b

11

PLATE 12 - This heavy ring of solid gold with a great elliptical head preserves several decorative elements which were typical of classic times. The finely modelled head of the winged youth and the female figures on either side of the head of the ring are reminiscent of Attic art, but their interpretation and especially the decorative expressionism of the whole jewel are peculiar to Etruscan art. Middle of 5th century B. C. Diameter 1 in.

BOLOGNA, Museo Civico. — FROM BOLOGNA, Sepolcreto della Certosa. — Bibliography: Ducati, *Mon. Ant.*, XX, 1910, col. 643; Id., *Guida*, p. 130; Id., *B. d. A.*, 1923, p. 509-511; Id., *A. E.*, p. 331; Id., *Bologna*, I, p. 26; Grenier, *Bologne*, p. 359; Becatti, n. 305, pl. LXXVI; *Ori Emilia*, n. 27, fig. 4-5-6; *Etruria Padana*, n. 696, pl. XI.

PLATE 13 a - Two earrings of oval, shield-like appearance, with hammered, filigreed and granulated decorations. Both the central bulges and the massive spheres at the bottom are over-decorated. 5th-4th centuries B. C. Height 2 ¹/₈ ins.

FLORENCE, Museo Archeologico (inventory no. 85036, 85036 bis). — FROM POPULONIA, acquired by Maruzzi in 1911. — Bibliography: *Mostra Scult. Etr.*, n. 115; *Mostra Etrusca*, n. 131; Becatti, n. 417 pl. CXI.

PLATE 13 b - Three simple parts of a necklace. Each part is a compressed sphere of laminated gold. Only the centre piece is decorated with a delicate motif of ivy leaves in the middle and cloves in relief on both sides. First half of 5th century B. C. Diameter 1 in.

FERRARA, Museo Archeologico Nazionale. — FROM VALLE TREBBIA. — Bibliography: *Ori Emilia*, n. 55-56.

Plate 12

12

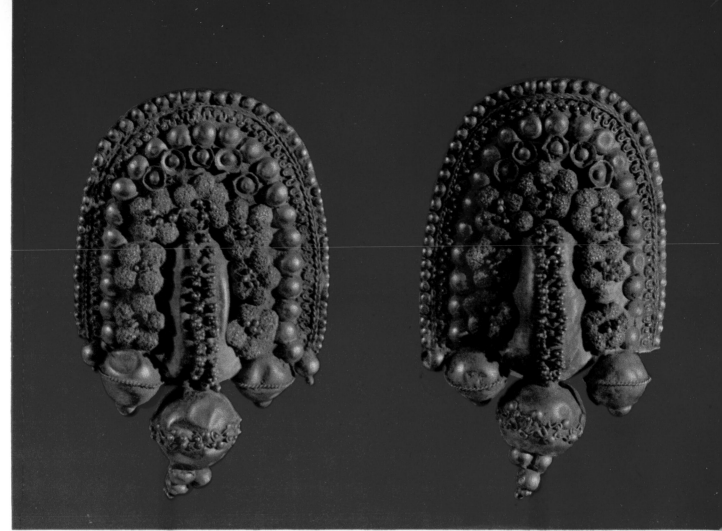

Plate 13 a

Plate 13 b

13

PLATE 14 - Detail of an earring of unusual shape, richly decorated with hammered and granulated motifs of flowers, and with discs and pearls. 5th century B. C. Height $^5/_8$ in.

FLORENCE, Museo Archeologico. — Provenance uncertain; passed through old collections. — Bibliography: K. Z., p. 152, n. 460; Fiumi, *St. Etr.*, XXV, p. 481, fig. 6.

PLATE 15 - From a delicately carved handle, this mirror opens out into a perfect circle with extremely accurate relief decorations. The scene represents three divinities whose names are lightly carved against the background: the seated figure at the left is Apollo (Apulu); at the centre is Jupiter (Tinia), the father of the gods, holding his sceptre; at the right Hermes (Turms) rests his caduceus against his side. End of 4th century B. C. Length 9 $^5/_8$ ins; diameter 3 $^7/_8$ ins.

FLORENCE, Museo Archeologico (inventory no. 74831). — FROM BOMARZO. — Bibliography: Milani, *RMA*, p. 143, pl. XXXVII; Ducati, *A. E.*, p. 448, fig. 524; Noll, *Jahreshefte*, XXVII, 1931, 1932, p. 159 ff., fig. 100; Mansuelli, *St Etr.*, XVI, p. 545, n. 2, pl. XLV; *Mostra Etrusca* n. 354.

Plate 15

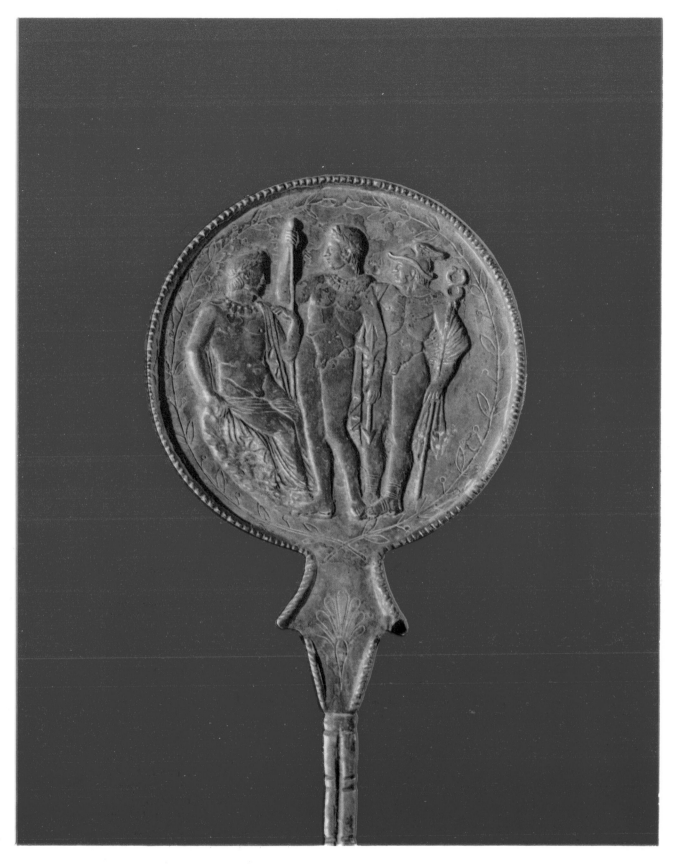

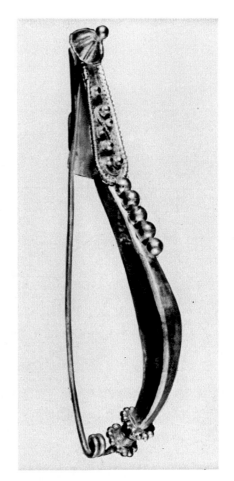

Plate 16 a   Plate 16 b

PLATE 16 a - Torques found in a Gallic burial ground. It consists of a simple cord with a knurled thread twisted around it. Beginning of 4th century B. C. Diameter 5 ¹/₈ ins.

> ANCONA, Museo Nazionale (inventory no. 1873). — FROM MONTE FORTINO DI AVERVIA (Ancona), Gallic burial ground, Tomb no. 23. — Bibliography: Brizio, *Mon. Ant.*, IX, 1899, coll. 681, 723, pl. V. 1; Marconi, *Itinerario*, n. 37, fig. p. 45.

PLATE 16 b - Arched fibula of a fairly simple type, but slightly more rigid than conventional ones and decorated with painstaking care. First half of 4th century B. C. Length 2 ³/₄ ins.

> BOLOGNA, Museo Civico. — FROM BOLOGNA, Palazzo delle Poste. — Bibliography: *Cart. Arch.*, f. 87, I, n. 17; *Ori Emilia*, n. 40, 41.

PLATE 17 - Two large earrings of hammered laminated gold. Their shape, an oval shield, stresses the different decorative aspect of the upper and lower parts: the upper is minutely and painstakingly executed as far as the man flanked by two sea-horses; the lower part is subjected to a broader treatment. The heads of two girls are visible above the five protruding pearls in the lower part of each earring. End of 4th-beginning of 3rd centuries B. C. Height 3 ⁵/₈ ins.

> FLORENCE, Museo Archeologico (inventory no. 15803, 15804). — Provenance uncertain; passed through old collections. — Bibliography: *Mostra Scult. Etr.*, n. 156; *Mostra Etrusca*, n. 136; Becatti, n. 415, pl. CXI.

Plate

16

PLATE 18 a - The central part of a necklace, consisting of two pendants, one *bulla,* and a few tubular elements. The pendants are decorated with hammered palm-trees and leaves; the *bulla* is composed of two shell-like pieces and depicts Perseus slaying Medusa. Beginning of 4th century B. C. Length of pendant 1 ¹/₈ ins.

ANCONA, Museo Nazionale (inventory no. 3470). — FROM S. FILIPPO DI OSIMO, Gallic burial ground, Tomb no. 4. — Bibliography: Dall'Osso, *Guida,* fig. p. 276; Moretti, *Dedalo,* V. p. 15, fig. p. 13; Marconi, *Itinerario,* n. 37, fig. p. 60; Andrén, *Opuscula Archaeologica,* V, 1948, p. 99.

PLATE 18 b - Necklace of small gold discs. The discs are convex and decorated with hammered rosettes and female faces portrayed frontally. 3rd century B. C. Diameter of discs 1 in.

ROME, Museo Villa Giulia (inventory *nos* 2737-2738). — FROM TODI. — Bibliography: Helbig, *Führer,* n. 1771; Bendinelli, *Mon. Ant.,* XXIII, col. 617, fig. 14, col. 619, fig. 7; Giglioli, *A. E.,* pl. CCCLXXV, 2.

PLATE 19 - Two lavishly decorated earrings. The main part of each jewel consists of an oblong, convex lamina bordered by a filigreed ivy-leaf pattern. A central pendant and four slim chains hang below the oblong, the pendant representing a female head with earrings and a large flower in the hair. At the lower end of the chains and pendant are a number of spindle-shaped smaller pendants. Beginning of 3rd century B. C. Length 4 ins.

ROME, Museo Villa Giulia (inventory no. 2731). — FROM TODI, Necropoli della Peschiera. — Bibliography: Helbig, *Führer,* n. 1771; Bendinelli, *Mon. Ant.* 23, 1911, c. 614, pl. I; Hadaczek, *Ohrschmuck,* p. 68, fig. 135; Ducati, *A. E.,* p. 514 fig. 616; Giglioli, *A. E.,* pl. CCCLXXV, 3; Becatti, n. 410.

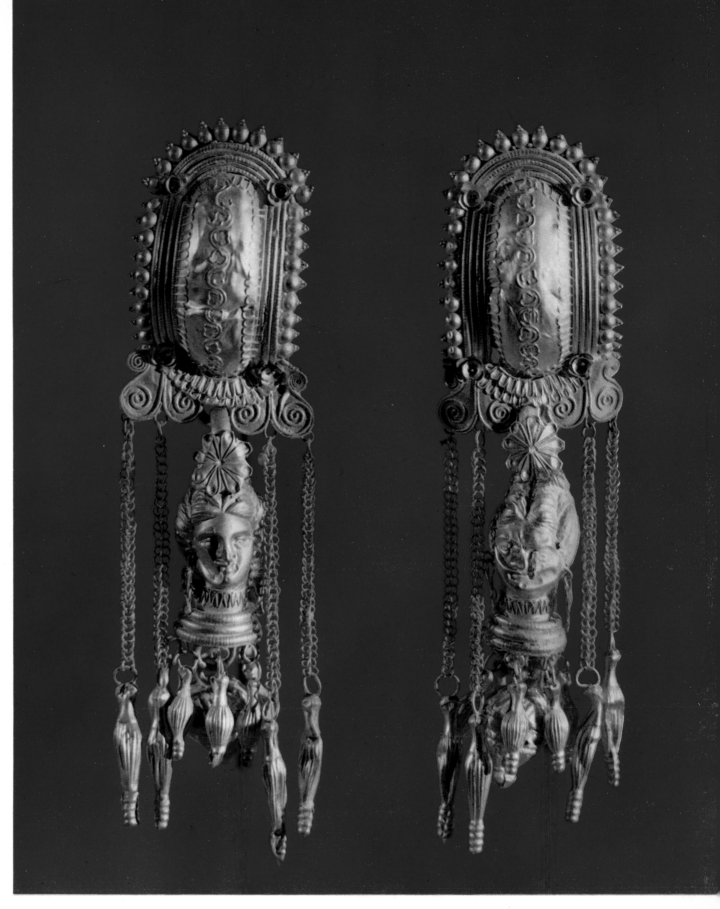

Plate 19

PLATE 20 a - Part of large necklace in gold lamina decorated with hammered palms and volutes. 4th century B. C. Diameter 1 ³/₈ ins.

ANCONA, Museo Nazionale (inventory no. 3677). — FROM FILOTTRANO (Ancona). — Bibliography: Dall'Osso, *Guida*, p. 22; Baumgärtel, *J.R.A.I.*, LXVII, 1937, p. 237, pl. XIX, 11 & 13.

PLATE 20 b - This, the central *bulla* of a necklace, portrays the head of a woman generously endowed with hair and wearing a necklace with pendants. We see here a typical example of Etruscan jewelry of the classic period, from the beginning of 4th century B. C. Diameter 1 in.

ANCONA, Museo Nazionale (inventory no. 3872). — FROM FILOTTRANO (Ancona), Gallic burial ground at S. Paolina, Tomb no. 9. — Bibliography: Dall'Osso, *Guida*, p. 264, fig. p. 234; Baumgärtel, *J.R.A.I.*, LXVII, 1937, p. 253, pl. XXIX, 7-9; Becatti, n. 363, pl. XCIII.

PLATE 21 a - Three slim chains are the components of this beautiful necklace. The central pendant is an onyx stone set in a gold granulate *bulla*. The two lateral pendants are stamped with a female head, frontally portrayed and strongly reminiscent of certain coins from Syracuse. The two ends of the entwined chains are linked by means of fourteen tubular sections. End of 4th — beginning of 3rd century B. C. Length 21 ⁵/₈ ins.

ROME, Museo Villa Giulia (inventory no. 2732). — FROM TODI. — Bibliography: Bendinelli, *Mon. Ant.*, XXXIII, col. 616; Ducati, *A. E.*, p. 515, fig. 618; Giglioli, *A. E.*, pl. CCCLXXV, 4; Becatti, n. 364.

PLATE 21 b - The pendants of this necklace represent the heads of sileni and maenads. The inspiration is classic but the motif is mechanically repeated and the whole composition is heavy. End of 4th — beginning of 3rd centuries B. C. Length of pendants 1 ⁵/₈ ins.

FLORENCE, Museo Archeologico Nazionale (inventory no. 15951). — FROM VOLTERRA, old collections. — Bibliography: *Mostra Scult. Etr.*, n. 159; *Mostra Etrusca*, n. 135; Becatti, n. 416, pl. CXI.

Plate 21

Plate 20 a

Plate 20 b

Plate 21

21

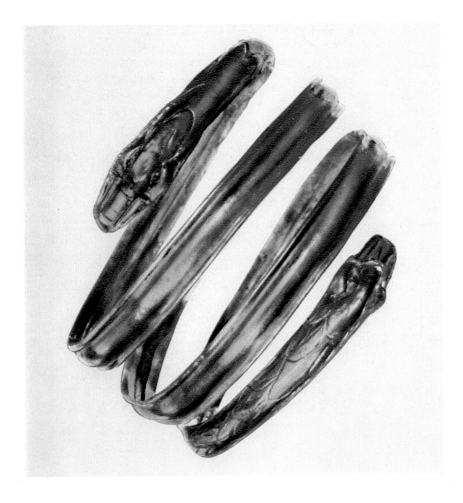

PLATE 22 - Spiral bracelet of laminated gold. The motif of a serpent's spires — originally a Greek invention — found a special interpretation in the hands of Etruscan craftsmen. They devised two serpents within one body but with a head at each end. 4th — 3rd centuries B. C. Diameter 2 ¹/₈ ins.

ANCONA, Museo Nazionale (inventory no. 1817). — FROM MONTEFORTINO. — Bibliography: Brizio, *Mon. Ant.*, IX, 1899, col. 667, 729, pl. III, 5; Dall'Osso, *Guida*, p. 217; Moretti *Dedalo*, V, p. 3, fig. 9; Ducati, *A. E.*, p. 518, pl. CCXXV, n. 622; Marconi, *Itinerario*, n. 37.

PLATE 23 a - The motif of a row of separate heads — but not mechanically repeated — reappears on this silver horsebuckle, probably used only during important military parades. The heads recall *têtes coupées* which, with the triskele, were typical Gallic manifestations and destined to appear again much later on the arches of Romanesque cathedrals. Diameter 7 ¹/₂ ins.

BRESCIA, Museo Romano. — FROM VILLA VECCHIA DI MANERBIO (Brescia), found in 1928. — Bibliography: Albizzati, *Historia*, VII, 1933, p. 570, 578; Schaffran, *Die Kunst der Langobarden*, p. 123 (wrongly attributed to Lombard art): Jacobsthal, *Early Celtic Art*, p. 124, n. 84, pls. LII, LIV; Laviosa-Zambotti, *Storia di Milano*, I, p. 108; Panazza, *Civici Musei*, p. 30; Mirabella Roberti, *Museo di Brescia*, p. 22.

PLATE 23 b - The Filottrano torques. The torques was worn by Gallic women round their necks. This splendid example should be considered an original Gallic piece from the Senonian territory brought to Italy during the first Celt invasions. 4th century B. C. Diameter 6 ins; weight 8 ozs.

ANCONA, Museo Nazionale (inventory no. 3679). — FROM FILOTTRANO, Gallic burial ground of S. Paolina, Tomb no. 2. — Bibliography: Marconi, *Itinerario, n.* 37, p. 21; Jacobsthal, *Early Celtic Art*, p. 170, n. 44, pl. XXXVIII.

Plate 23 a

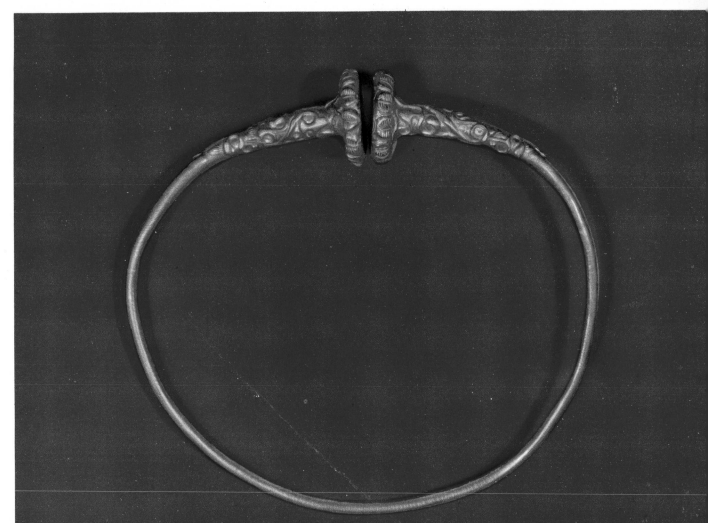

Plate 23 b

Plate 25

Plate 24

PLATE 24 - These tubular containers have lids surmounted by heads of lions or hawks. They were found in Sardinia. They are of obvious Egyptian influence and did in fact contain rolled laminae with engraved figures exactly similar to those in the Egyptian Book of the Dead. Typical of the Phoenician phase (550 B. C.). Height ³/₈ in.

> CAGLIARI, Museo Nazionale. — FROM THARROS. — Bibliography: Marshall, n. 1560 ff; Cara, *Tharros e Cornus*, p. 15; Pesce, *Sardegna Punica*, p. 115.

PLATE 25 a - The armlet is composed of five hinged laminae, decorated with hammered symbols. The central part shows a winged scarab holding a disc between its upper antennae, and a ringed object between its legs. Granulation is used here to stress the details and contours of the design. The other laminae are decorated with stylized palm and lotus leaves. 7th — 6th centuries B. C. Length 5 ins; height 1 ³/₈ ins.

> CAGLIARI, Museo Nazionale (inventory no. 21628). — FROM THARROS, found in a Punic tomb. in the 19th century. Serralutzu Collection. — Bibliography: Taramelli, *Museo di Cagliari*, p. 56; cfr. Marshall; Becatti, n. 227.

PLATE 25 b - These two earrings, though obviously of the same type, reveal differences in execution. The upper part of the one on the left is in the form of a perfect half-moon; its counterpart on the right is leech-shaped. However, the birds or hawks below are practically identical and the same may be said of the two acorn-shaped pendants. 7th — 6th centuries B. C. Length 2 ³/₄ ins. and 3 ⁵/₈ ins.

> CAGLIARI, Museo Nazionale. — FROM THARROS, found in a Punic tomb. — Bibliography: Perrot-Chipiez, III, p. 818, figs, 517 & 577; cfr. Taramelli, *Museo di Cagliari*, p. 56; Becatti, n. 221, pl. XLI; Pesce, *Sardegna punica*, p. 113.

Plate 25

PLATE 26 - A very decorative necklace of gold and yellow amber, with small discs alternating with pearls. The centre of each disc was set with grains of amber and granulated triangles. 8th — 7th centuries B. C. Length 12 1/4 ins.

NAPLES, Museo Archeologico Nazionale (inventory no. 126418). — FROM CUMA, Fondo Maiorana, in a trench tomb. — Bibliography: Gabrici, *Mon. Ant.*, XXII, 1913, col. 294-295; Breglia, n. 13, pl. I, 3; Siviero n. 4, pls. VI-VII.

PLATE 27 a - Small gold rosette of six lobes inside which smaller rosettes are alternated with hammered female heads. At the centre another rosette with granulated borders is inserted into a seven-point star. Rhodian art. 7th — 6th centuries B. C. Diameter 1 3/8 ins.

BOLOGNA, Museo Civico, Palagi Collection. — Bibliography: Ducati, *Guida*, p. 70; Rosemberg, *Granulation*, p. 73, fig. 121; Becatti, n. 202, pl. XXXIV; *Ori Emilia*, n. 265, fig. 76.

PLATE 27 b - Two rings with " eye-shaped " oval heads, one decorated with a cow feeding her calf, the other with a snarling wolf. The deep impression left by the engraver's tool shows that these jewels were used as seals. 6th — 5th centuries B. C. Diameters of ring: 5/8 in. and 1/2 ins; diameters of heads: 1 3/8 ins and 1 3/8 x 5/8 ins.

SYRACUSE, Museo Archeologico Nazionale (inventory nos. 46517 and 45905). — FROM S. ANGELO MUXARO (Agrigento). — Bibliography: Becatti, n. 303-302.

Plate 27 a

Plate 27 b

27

Plate 28

PLATE 28 - Necklace in laminated gold with bivalvular grains and pendants. The female masks on the pendants were obtained by means of a punch. The smile on their faces recalls early Hellenic art. 6th century B. C. Weight 6 ¹/₂ drams.

TARANTO, Museo Nazionale (inventory no. 6429). — FROM RUVO, acquired by Caldarola. — Bibliography: Breglia, *Japigia*, X, 1939, n. 1, fig. 1; Becatti, n. 272, a, b.

PLATE 29 - This necklace, found at Ruvo, may well be considered one of the most elegant jewels of antiquity. A ribbon of flexible lace supports a net of mail festooned with lotus flowers, acorns and masks of Silenus. The pendants are in stamped lamina, but the capsules of the acorns and the calyxes of the lotus flowers are granulated. A similar, but more subtle treatment has been applied to the hair of the sileni. The numerous elements in this work, far from creating an impression of confusion or exaggeration, are perfectly balanced and harmonized. 6th — 5th centuries B. C. Length 12 ⁵/₈ ins.

NAPLES, Museo Archeologico Nazionale (inventory no. 24883). — FROM RUVO, acquired by Ficco. — Bibliography: Ruggiero, *Scavi di Antichità*, p. 563; Breglia, n. 22, pl. III, 1; Siviero, n. 34, pls. XXXIV, XXXVII; Becatti, n. 273, pl. CCLXXIII a-b.

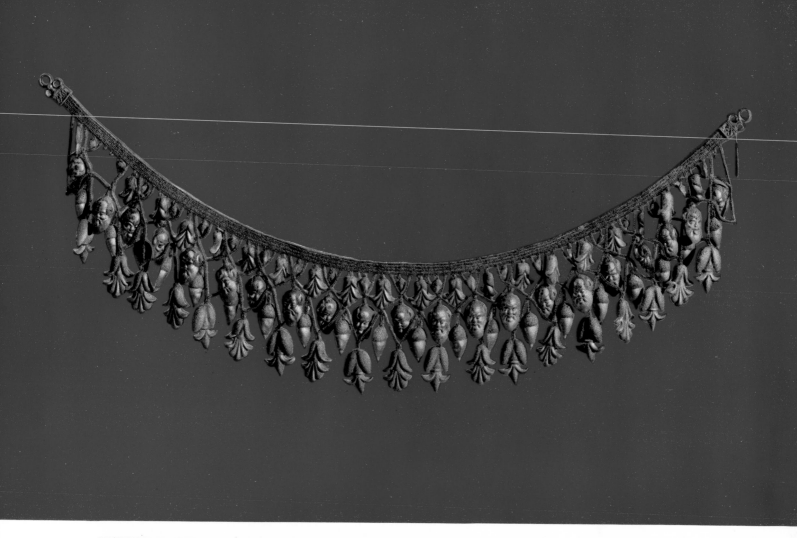

Plate 29

Plate 29
(detail)

Plate 30

PLATE 30 - Supports for balm-burners like this one are typical products from Ruvo. They consist of simple cylinders with a very wide brim. The type reproduced here is decorated with two hammered concentric rows of volutes and gorgons. 6th century B. C. Height 1 ⁷/₈ ins; diameter 3 ¹/₂ ins.

> NAPLES, Museo Archeologico Nazionale. — FROM RUVO, acquired by Ficco. — Bibliography: Ruggiero, *Scavi di Ant.*, p. 563; Breglia n. 47; Siviero, n. 23.

PLATE 31 - Trapezoid pendant of stamped gold lamina. Within the lightly engraved borders a running hare surmounts five rosettes. Beneath the lamina are three decorated pendants in the shape of lotus flowers. 6th century B. C. Total height 3 ³/₈ ins.

> BARI, Museo Archeologico (inventory no. 1659). — FROM MOICATTARO. — Bibliography: Mayer, *Apulien*, p. 282, pl. XXIII, 5.

30

Plate 31

PLATE 32 a - Discoid earrings with pendants in the shape of reversed cones. The discs are decorated with filigreed roses and palms, and the pendants with a spiral thread of small beads. 4th century B. C. Diameter of discs ⁵/₈ in.; height of cones 1 ⁵/₈ ins.

TARANTO, Museo Nazionale (inventory no. 22407 A-B). — FROM GINOSA, found in a tomb in the Girifalco district. — Bibliography: Breglia, *Japigia*, X, 1939, n. 13, fig. 8; Becatti, n. 389, a, b, c.

PLATE 32 b - Detail of the clasp of a necklace of flattened gold mail decorated with filigreed leaves and small palms. 4th century B. C. Total length 16 ³/₄ ins.

TARANTO, Museo Nazionale (inventory no. 54116). — FROM MOTTOLA. — Bibliography: Becatti, n. 429.

Plate 32 a

Plate 32 b

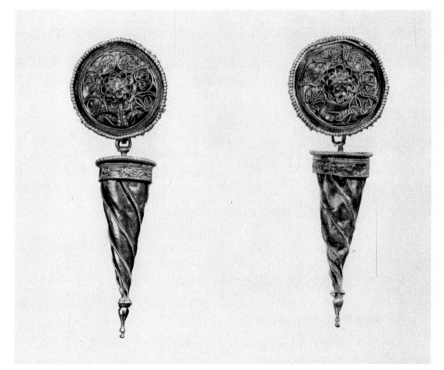

PLATE 33 - The motif of the " Knot of Hercules " seems to have become fashionable among Taranto jewelers during the 4th century B. C. It was believed to have magic powers and to ward off evil. This example from Ginosa, possibly part of a diadem, is decorated with an extremely delicate filigree of roses and palms. 4th century B. C. Height 1 in; width ³/₄ in.

TARANTO, Museo Nazionale (inventory no. 22406). — FROM GINOSA. — Bibliography: Breglia, *Japigia*, X, 1939, n. 24, fig. 13; Becatti, n. 384.

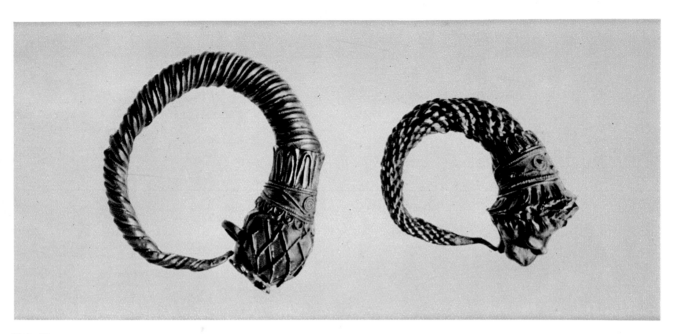

Plate 34

PLATE 34 - The motif of a lion's head, with its mane forming rays, is frequently repeated in Italiot jewelry, though it is also found in Etruscan production. One finds it in armlets, in chain clasps and especially in earrings. These examples from Sicily are similar to several others found in the Taranto area, which would support the theory that they were mass-produced in a local factory. 4th century B. C. Height ⁷/₈ in. and 1 ³/₈ ins.

SYRACUSE, Museo Archeologico Nazionale (inventory nos. 39769 - 35036). — FROM CAVA D'ISPICA AND TERRAVECCHIA DI GRAMMICHELE.

PLATE 35 a - This splendid example of diadems from Taranto is decorated with seven separately fashioned roses fixed to a simple gold band. Its date is suggested by the presence of 4th century B. C. vases from Apulia found during the same excavations. Diameter 6 ins; width of roses 1 ⁵/₈ ins.

TARANTO, Museo Nazionale (inventory no. 6469). — FROM CARBONARA (Bari), accidental discovery. — Bibliography: Breglia, *Japigia*, X, 1939, n. 11, fig. 6; Becatti, n. 351.

PLATE 35 b - The decorative scheme of these two disc-shaped earrings was to become very fashionable during the exuberant Hellenistic period. The small female heads are perfectly rounded and composed of two laminae welded together. They too wear earrings and a diadem. 4th century B. C. Diameter of discs 1 in; total height 2 ³/₈ ins.

TARANTO, Museo Nazionale (inventory no. 54115 A-B). — FROM CRISPIANO. — Bibliography: Becatti, n. 388 a-b.

Plate 35 a

Plate 35 b

Plate 36

PLATE 36 - This jeweler from Taranto conceived two doves as pendants to his disc-shaped earrings. The wings are in gold laminae and the feathers are granulated. 3rd century B. C. Height 1 ³/₅ ins.

TARANTO, Museo Nazionale (inventory no. 64430 A-B). — FROM TARANTO, Necropolis of Piazza d'Armi, Tomb no. 4. — Bibliography: Breglia, *Japigia*, X, 1939, n. 19, p. 18 ff.

PLATE 37 a - Twisted bracelet with rams' heads at each end. 4th century B. C. Diameter 2 ³/₄ ins.

TARANTO, Museo Nazionale (inventory no. 54118). — FROM MOTTOLA (Taranto). — Bibliography: Becatti, n. 373 a-b.

PLATE 37 b - The female head on this heavy ring from Taranto has its hair arranged in the typical "melon" style of the women sculptured by Praxiteles. The facial features and traditional details recall the provincial Italiot taste reflected in locally produced painted pottery of the 4th century B. C. Diameter of surface 1 ¹/₈ x 1 in, diameter of ring 1 in.

TARANTO, Museo Nazionale (inventory no. 54117). — FROM MOTTOLA (Taranto), found in a tomb. — Bibliography: Becatti, n. 334.

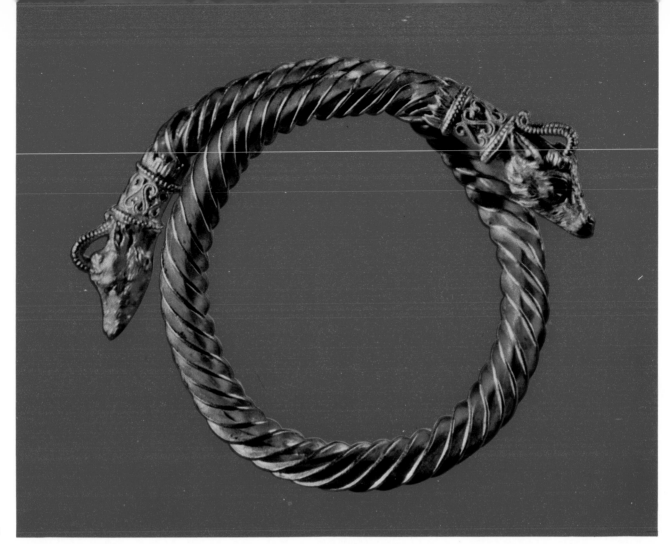

Plate 37 a

Plate 37 b

Plate 38

PLATE 38 - Coiled earring of hollow lamina with two-faced heads at each end. 4th century B. C. Height 1 in; width 1 in.

> TARANTO, Museo Nazionale (inventory no. 12036). — FROM TARANTO, accidental discovery during road-works in Via Principe Amedeo. — Bibliography: Breglia, *Japigia*, X, 1939, n. 15; Becatti, n. 380.

PLATE 39 a - Two exquisite examples of the Taranto school. In the upper half of the picture is part of an armlet, the clasp of which consists of two lions' heads confronting each other and very finely engraved; in the lower half are two earrings of spiralled gold thread, also decorated with heads of lions. Second half of 4th century B. C. Diameter of armlet 2 ³/₄ ins; length of earrings 1 in.

> TARANTO, Museo Nazionale (inventory nos. 6432 and 6434 A-B). — FROM TARANTO. — Bibliography: Breglia, *Japigia*, X, 1939, n. 40 & n. 41-42; Becatti, n. 374 a, b.

PLATE 39 b - The excellent jeweler from Taranto who executed this diadem experimented successfully with two techniques. He hammered the bush of acanthus out of the lamina and filigreed the flowering shoots and campanulae in the background. The resulting decorative effect is delightful. 4th - 3rd centuries B. C. Length 4 ³/₄ ins; width ³/₄ in.

> TARANTO, Museo Nazionale (inventory no. 54114). — FROM CRISPIANO (Taranto). — Bibliography: Becatti, n. 347.

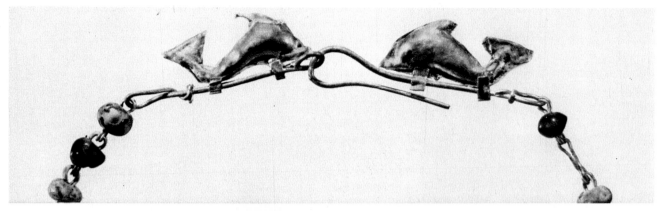

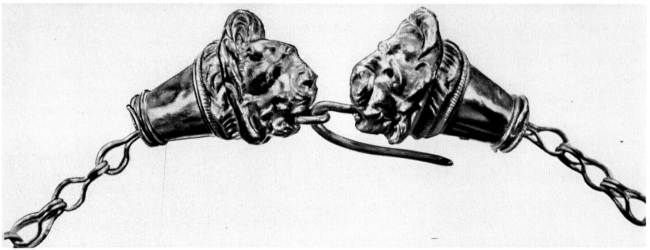

Plate 40

PLATE 40 - Although he may have been commissioned only to execute a simple necklace, the craftsman from Taranto would use his talent on the clasp. Here are two examples of typical figures: the lion and the dolphin. 4th — 3rd centuries B. C.

    TARANTO, Museo Nazionale (inventory nos. 6433, 22410). — FROM TARANTO. — Bibliography: Breglia *Japigia*, X, 1939, fig. 22 & n. 39; Becatti, n. 374.

PLATE 41 a - Two fibulae in the shape of lions. The animals were fashioned by hammering and welding two laminae; the details of the manes and bodies are apparently carved with a burin. The other half of each fibula is decorated with filigreed designs and gadroons. 4th century B. C. Length 2 ¹/₈ ins. and 1 ⁷/₈ ins.

    LECCE, Museo Provinciale Castromediano (inventory nos. 3897, 3898). — FROM ROCA VECCHIA. — Bibliography: Bernardini, *Not. Sc.* 1934, p. 196.

PLATE 41 b - The decorative motifs of this long terracotta frieze, coated with gold and destined for a funereal resting place, are the fight between a member of the Arimaspi people and two griffins (reproduced in this plate) and the fight between a griffin and a horse. End of 4th — beginning of 3rd centuries B. C. Average height 2 ³/₄ ins; average length 4 ³/₈ ins.

    TARANTO, Museo Nazionale (inventory no. 5435). — FROM TARANTO, found in a tomb between Via D'Alò and Via Messapia. — Bibliography: Bernabò Brea, *Not. Sc.*, 1940, p. 453, n. 23, fig. 29.

Plate 41 a

Plate 41 b

41

PLATE 43 a - An extremely light, elegant diadem of oak leaves, consisting of a thin stamped lamina. In the centre of the jewel is a flower with folded petals. 3rd century B. C. Diameter 6 ³/₄ ins.

TARANTO, Museo Nazionale (inventory no. 6472). — FROM TARANTO.

PLATE 43 b - One of the most famed masterpieces of the Taranto school is this diadem, decorated with flowers and consisting of a band spiralling round a gold laminated support. Small filigreed flowers, set off by enamels and bright precious stones (see plate 42) represent the decorative element of this splendid jewel, once the proud possession of a young girl from Messapia. 3rd century B. C. Diameter 5 ⁷/₈ ins; maximum length 6 ³/₄ ins.

TARANTO, Museo Nazionale (inventory no. 22437). — FROM CANOSA. — Bibliography: Bartoccini, *Japigia*, VI, 1935, p. 248-254, fig. 13-15; Becatti, n. 353.

Plate 43

Plate 42

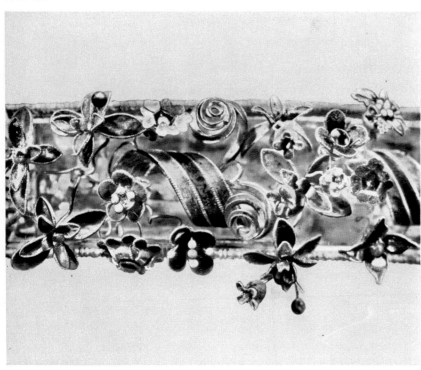

Plate 43

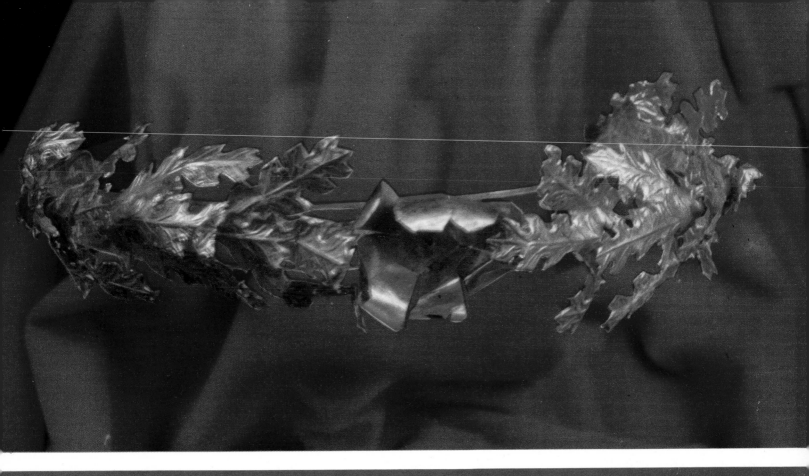

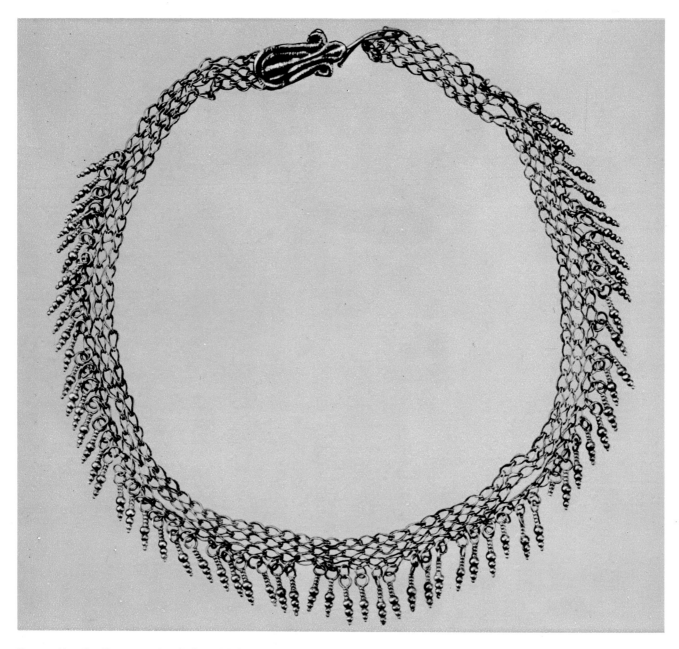

PLATE 44 - In the same tomb in which the diadem (plate 43 b) was found was this gold necklace consisting of three strings of chain-mail decorated with a fringe of pendants. These are small stamped droplets. Length 13 ³/₈ ins.

TARANTO, Museo Nazionale (inventory no. 22438). — FROM CANOSA. — Bibliography: Bartoccini, *Japigia*, VI, 1935, p. 254, fig. 17.

PLATE 45 - The tomb also contained a jewel-box and the inscription carved on the upper lip of the hinge bears the name of the young woman whose grave her bereaved parents filled with treasures. Her name was Opakas-Sabalidas. The box consists of two halves forming a shell. The upper half is decorated with a nereid riding a sea-dragon; in the lower shell the same figure is seen frontally, sitting on a sea-lioness. Note the elegant waves stylized into volutes, the dragon's scales and ruby eye, and the nereid's delicate hair. 3rd century B. C. Diameter 5 ⁵/₈ ins.

TARANTO, Museo Nazionale (inventory no. 22430). — FROM CANOSA. — Bibliography: Bartoccini, *Japigia*, VI, 1935, p. 230, fig. 4-5 Becatti, n. 446 a-b.

Plate 45

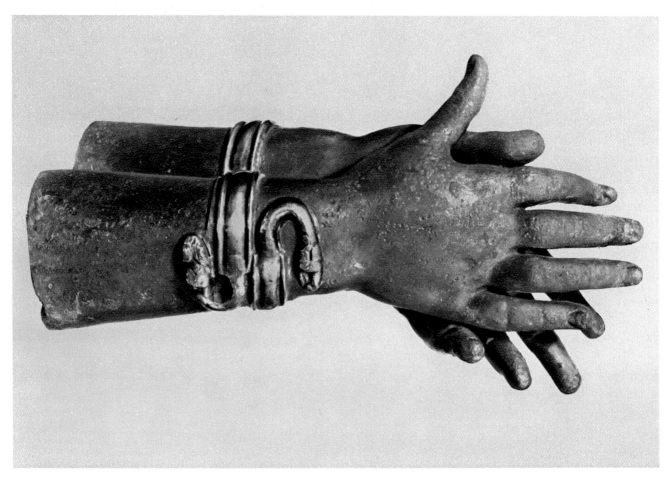

Plate 46

PLATE 46 - These two female forearms in molten bronze bear around each wrist a bracelet of gold lamina with a snake's head at both ends. The function and destination of this object have not been clearly established but, as the forearms are hinged, and the hands can be clasped or unclasped, it may have been a nutcracker. 3rd — 2nd centuries B. C. Length 6 ins.

TARANTO, Museo Nazionale (inventory no. 22631). — FROM TARANTO (Rondinella district), Tomb no. 4 (sarcophagus). — Bibliography: Becatti, n. 497.

PLATE 47 - This heavy oil-lamp of laminated gold, decorated with hammered flowers and bean-shaped designs is the first object on show to have been found in the Campania region, near the great centres of Pompei and Ercolano. 1st century B. C. — 1st century A. D. Height 5 7/8 ins; diameter 6 1/2 ins.

NAPLES, Museo Archeologico Nazionale (inventory no. 25000). — FROM POMPEI. — Bibliography: Brunn, *Bull. Corr. Arch.,* 1863, p. 90-91; Breglia, n. 1025, pl. XLIV, 1; Siviero, n. 341, pls. CCVI - CCIX.

Plate

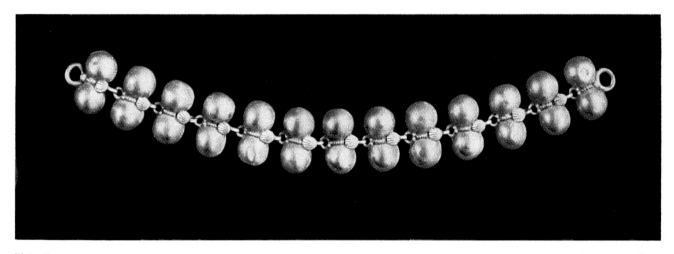

Plate 48

PLATE 48 - This armlet consists of half-spheres of laminated gold held together by gadrooned threads, with small sea-shells in the links. 1st century B. C. — 1st century A. D. Length 9 ¼ ins.

NAPLES, Museo Archeologico Nazionale (inventory no. 110919). — FROM POMPEI. — Bibliography: *Not. Sc.*, 1876, p. 146; Breglia, n. 865-866; Siviero, n. 246, pl. CLXXVIII a.

PLATE 49 - One of the most beautiful necklaces discovered in the Pompei area. Alternating along a strip of gold-mail, a series of emeralds and slabs of mother-of-pearl create a delicate and most effective chromatic display. The large clasp at the top is decorated with an emerald. 1st century B. C. — 1st century A. D. Length 13 ⅝ ins.

NAPLES, Museo Archeologico Nazionale (inventory no. 113576). — FROM POMPEI, discovered in the Bottaro district, fondo Valiante, on January 18, 1881. — Bibliography: *Not. Sc.*, 1881, p. 27; Breglia, n. 473, pl. XXXI, 2; Siviero, n. 164, pl. CXXXIII.

Plate 49

Plate 50

PLATE 50 - This simple, extremely elegant necklace of small oak leaves with deeply engraved nervations was discovered together with the necklace reproduced in the previous plate. The clasp at the centre, in the shape of a disc, might have enabled the necklace to be used also as a belt. 1st century B. C. — 1st century A. D. Length 40 $^1/_2$ ins.

NAPLES, Museo Archeologico Nazionale (inventory nos. 111113, 111114). — Bibliography: *Not. Soc.*, 1877, p. 128; Breglia, n. 477-478, pl. XXXVI, 2; Siviero, n. 166, pls. CXXXIV - CXXXV.

PLATE 51 - Flat spiralled armlet with a snake's head and tail, engraved in the fashionable manner of the Hellenistic period. The snake's eyes, wich must have been glass-paste, imparted absolute realism to the composition. 1st century B. C. — 1st century A. D.

NAPLES, Museo Archeologico Nazionale (inventory no. 24824). — FROM POMPEI. — Bibliography: Museo Borbonico, VII, pl. XLVI; Breglia, n. 827, pl. XXVII, 3; Siviero, n. 202, pl. CLVI; Becatti, n. 499.

50

Plate 51

PLATE 52 a - Here are some examples of what we have called " family silver ". Splendid, finely decorated drinking cups, with vegetable motifs and figures engraved all around. This " Kantaros " is decorated with bas-reliefs on a background of masks, thyrsi and vases. 1st century B. C. — 1st century A. D. Height 4 ³/₈ ins; diameter 4 ³/₈ ins.

NAPLES, Museo Archeologico Nazionale (inventory no. 25380).

PLATE 52 b - This cup, portraying Mars and Venus, reveals decorative insistence in the vegetable element, used to fill in empty spaces. The effect, however, is not unattractive. Height 4 ⁵/₈ ins; width ⁷/₈ in; weight 1 lb. 2 ozs.

NAPLES, Museo Archeologico Nazionale (inventory no. 145515). — FROM POMPEI, House of Menander. — Bibliography: Maiuri, *La Casa del Menandro e il suo tesoro di argenteria*, Rome 1932, p. 321, pls. XXXI - XXXXIII.

PLATE 53 - Silver drinking cup with its body and handles enveloped by a delicate shoot of ivy and berries. The movement of each leaf and the resulting chiaroscuro effect brings out the fresh naturalistic quality of this object. 1st century B. C. — 1st century A. D. Height 4 ³/₄ ins; diameter 4 ³/₈ ins.

NAPLES, Museo Archeologico Nazionale (inventory no. 25379). — FROM ERCOLANO.

Plate 52 a

Plate 52 b

Plate 54

PLATE 54 - The mistress of the House of Menander had, among her jewelry, these earrings, reproduced from four different sets. The spherical one, of classic shape, was once enlivened with " eyes " of garnet. The others are more naturalistic in that they represent small bunches of grapes, variously composed of pearls, emeralds and globules of gold. 1st century B. C. — 1st century A. D. Heights: 1 ^{3}/$_8$ ins; 1 ^{1}/$_8$ ins; 1 ^{1}/$_8$ ins.

NAPLES, Museo Archeologico Nazionale. — FROM POMPEI, House of Menander. — Bibliography: Maiuri, op. cit., p. 380, n. 119, n. 120, n. 121; pl. LXV; Breglia, ns. 236, 237, 238, 239, 246, 247, pl. XXXIII, 5-6, 3-4; Siviero, n. 283, pls. CLXXXIX - CXCI, n. 284, pls. CLXXXIX - CXCI, n. 281, pls. CLXXXVIII - CLXXXIX.

PLATE 55 - This exceptionally beautiful mirror, decorated with a stern female head, is one of the many treasures found in the House of Menander, so called because a fresco of the great Attic poet was found there. Every detail and contour of this piece, especially the treatment of the hair, reveals the hand of a master-engraver, and echoes the motifs of Neoclassic Hellenism. Height 13 ^{5}/$_8$ ins; diameter 8 ^{1}/$_4$ ins; weight 1 lb. 10 ozs.

NAPLES, Museo Archeologico Nazionale (inventory no. 145524). — FROM POMPEI, House of Menander. — Bibliography: Maiuri, op. cit., p. 350, pl. XLVII.

Plate 55

PLATE 56 a - Oval silver dish. The border is decorated with scenes of grazing goats. Maximum diameter 9 $^{7}/_{8}$ ins; shorter diameter 4 $^{5}/_{8}$ ins.

TURIN, Museo di Antichità (inventory no. 5417).

PLATE 56 b - Handle of a shallow silver dish decorated with landscapes surmounted by a figure of Hermes. 1st — 2nd centuries A. D. Diameter 3 $^{1}/_{2}$ ins; length 3 $^{3}/_{8}$ ins.

TURIN, Museo di Antichità (inventory no. 5423).

PLATE 57 - Bust of Emperor Lucius Verus. This object was part of what we have described as the "hidden treasure" discovered at Marengo, near Alessandria. It is a completely rounded bust of thin silver lamina with no trace of welding. Each feature is minutely and lovingly executed by means of hammer and burin. However, in spite of the accurate treatment, it is a provincial work, revealing emphasis on traditional elements despite four centuries of Roman rule in the Po valley. 2nd century A. D. Total height 21 $^{7}/_{8}$ ins; maximum width 20 $^{1}/_{2}$ ins.

TURIN, Museo di Antichità (inventory no. 5450). — FROM MARENGO (Alessandria), accidentally dug up in 1928. — Bibliography: Bendinelli, *Il Tesoro di Marengo*, p. 33, pl. V.

Plate 56 a

Plate 56 b

Plate 57

PLATE 58 - This band of gold-plated silver was possibly part of a sword-belt. It includes thirteen high-relief figures of divinities. Its style and technique are typical of the special attention given in the Antonine era to prototypes and motifs of the Hellenistic period. 2nd century A. D. Length 33 $^{1}/_{2}$ ins; height 4 $^{5}/_{8}$ ins.

TURIN, Museo di Antichità (inventory n. 5457). — FROM MARENGO (Alessandria). — Bibliography: Bendinelli, *op. cit.*, p. 19, pls. VII, VIII.

PLATE 59 - A bell-shaped silver bowl, hammered and finished with a burin. It is surrounded by a double row of acanthus and other lanceolated leaves. Next to it is a " pulvinar ", probably part of a couch or circus seat, decorated with hammered spirals of acanthus leaves and shoots encircling a nude maenad. 2nd century. A. D. Height of bowl 6 $^{5}/_{8}$ ins; diameter of brim 8 $^{5}/_{8}$ ins; diameter of base 4 $^{3}/_{8}$ ins. Pulvinar: maximum height 14 $^{3}/_{8}$ ins; length 22 $^{1}/_{2}$ ins.

TURIN, Museo di Antichità (inventory no. 5458). — FROM MARENGO (Alessandria). — Bibliography: Bendinelli, *op. cit.*, p. 32 & p. 55, pl. XII.

Plate 58

58

Plate 59

PLATE 60 - The insertion of an imperial coin in necklace pendants, though certainly not a new practice, became popular among the late-ancient jewelers. This coin with the profile of Theodosius, attached to a gold chain, and found at Settimo (Pavia), helps us to establish the date of the jewel: 4th century A. D. Approximate length 17 ³/₄ ins.

PAVIA, Museo Civico. — FROM SETTIMO, found with other coins of 4th century A. D.

PLATE 61 - These three heavy rings, rather baroque in taste, are typical of the so-called late-ancient period. They were discovered with several other objects at Parma, and may be considered as a triumph of gold in all its chromatic splendour. Of the two rings lying horizontally, the one at left is decorated on left and right with spiralled motifs in black enamel; the centre-piece of the other ring is engraved with a warrior putting on his arms. The flowers and meanders on the gold body of this ring are punched through. Diameter 1 in; length of stone ³/₄ in; width ⁵/₈ in; Diameter 1 ¹/₈ ins; Diameter ³/₄ in; length of stone ³/₈ in; width ³/₈ in.

PARMA, Museo di Antichità. — FROM PARMA, Tesoro del Teatro Regio — Bibliography: De Lama, n. 5, pl. II, n. 6, pl. II; *Ori Emilia,* n. 147, fig. 44, pl. II; n. 146, fig. 44, n. 148, fig. 44, pl. II.

Plate 6

Plate 63

PLATE 62 - Spherical scent-container resting on a conical base. Four little chains hang from the square lid of the container, which can also be opened by a hinge. The object was decorated with fourteen cut amethysts. 5th century A. D. Height 2 $^1/_8$ ins; diameter 1 $^3/_8$ ins; weigth 1 $^1/_2$ ozs.

TURIN, Museo Civico di Palazzo Madama. — FROM DESANA (Vercelli). — Bibliography: Viale, *Boll. Storico Bibl. Sub.*, XLIII, 1941, p. 23, fig. 26.

PLATE 63 a - The Desana treasure represents the transition from the classic approach which still dominated the shapes of objects to the *nouvelle vague* technique of fretwork. This fibula may be considered one of the most ancient examples of this particular technique, which was ultimately to develop into the style of Byzantine and Gothic-Lombard jewelry. The hexagonal cells holding precious stones or pieces of coloured glass consisted of small blades welded to a slim gold lamina by means of the *cloisonné* technique. Observe the original invention of the four stylized heads of birds protruding at the left.

FROM DESANA (Vercelli). — Bibliography: Viale, *Boll. Storico Bibl. Sub.*, XLIII, 1941, p. 152; Becatti, n. 547, pl. 153.

PLATE 63 b - This magnificent jewel, also part of the Desana treasure, has been classified as an armlet. However, more recent studies — and the fact that during the 5th century women were forbidden to bare their arms — support the theory that it was in fact worn as a diadem. Inside the filigreed network a large oval amethyst is framed by four small garnets and four emeralds. An amethyst, an onyx and two garnets decorate the lateral strips of which only the one on the left has survived in its entirety. 4th — 5th centuries A. D.

TURIN, Museo Civico di Palazzo Madama. — FROM DESANA (Vercelli). — Bibliography: Viale, *Boll. Storico Bibl.*, XLIII, 1941, p. 151, fig. 21.

Plate 63

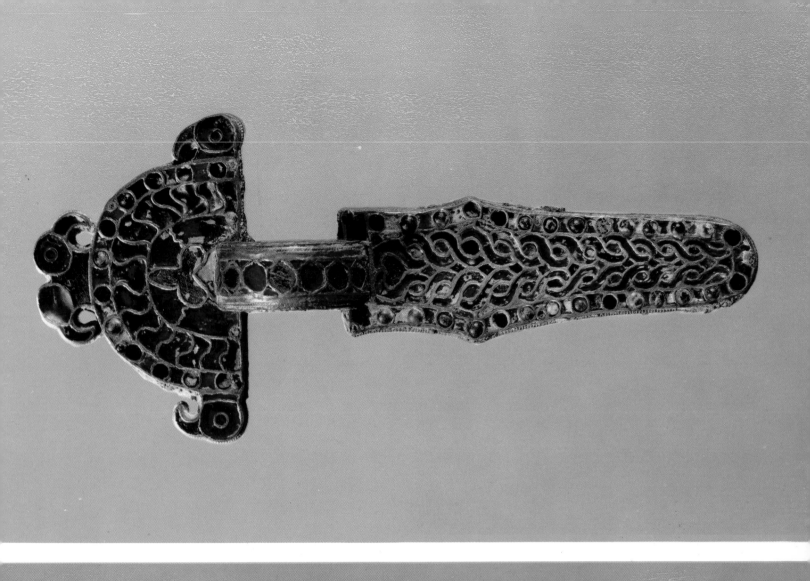

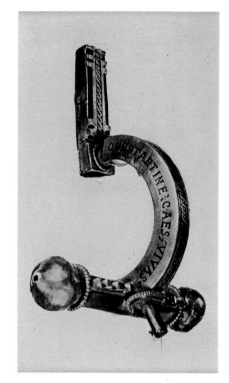

Plate 64 a   Plate 64 b

PLATE 64 a - In ancient times people used two types of spoons for liquid or semi liquid food:
the " Cochlear ", so called because it was used to eat from sea-shells (*cochleae*), and *the*
" Ligula ". The " Cochlear " had a rounded tip at the upper end to help push the food out of
the shell. Reproduced here are two examples, both bearing an inscription of welcome for
guests. 5th century A. D. Length 7 ³/₈ ins.

    TURIN, Museo Civico di Palazzo Madama. — FROM DESANA. — Bibliography: Viale, *op. cit.*, p. 29, fig. 39.

PLATE 64 b - Hinged fibula of the Latin Cross type with buttons at both ends of the horizontal
bar. The vertical clasp is decorated with an entwined motif and the arched part bears the
double inscription: COSTANTINE CAES VIVAS; HERCVLI CAES VINCAS. 4th century A. D.
Length 2 ³/₈ ins.

    TURIN, Museo di Antichità (inventory no. 5485).

PLATE 65 - The Parabiago dish. This splendid example of Roman lathe-work is remarkable for
the scene carved on it, dominated by the figure of the Great Mother Cybele, seated with Attis
in a chariot drawn by four lions. Three corybantes dance around them; on the right an
Atlas-like figure supports a solar divinity standing inside the Zodiacal belt. Above, the Sun chariot
follows that of the Moon, each respectively preceded by Vesper and Hesper. Below, the divinities
of Earth, Water and Hades are symbolically connected by four cherubs representing the Seasons.
This composition, if not perfectly rhythmical, is none the less plastic and effective, and has its
origins in Eastern Hellenism. However, the pictorial quality of the scenes and the representational elements have an unmistakable Roman flavour. It is difficult to establish the exact date of
this work of art which may have been created either in the 2nd-3rd century of the Empire, or
in the 4th century. Diameter 15 ³/₈ ins; weight 7 ³/₄ lbs.

    FROM PARABIAGO (Milan). — Bibliography: Levi, *La patera di Parabiago;* Alföldi, *Atlantis.*

Plate 65

PLATE 66 - Silver capsella (reliquary box) of elliptical shape, discovered in 1871 in the course of excavations beneath the main altar of Grado Basilica. It is decorated with hammered figures and inscriptions. The slightly convex surface shows a series of medallions with the figures, among others, of Christ, St. Peter and St. Paul. On the lid a bejeweled cross is flanked by two lambs. The treatment of these figures, already typically Christian, recalls in more than one way, similar representations in ivory. 5th century A. D. (?) Length 4 ⁵/₈ ins; width at centre 2 ⁵/₈ ins; height 3 ¹/₂ ins.

GRADO, Treasure of the Basilica. — Bibliography: Caprin, *Le Lagune di Grado*, 1890, p. 243; De Rossi, *Le insigni capselle reliquiarie scoperte a Grado;* Garrucci, *Storia dell'Arte Cristiana*, Prato, 1880, VI, p. 55-56; Morassi, *Antica Oreficeria in Italia*, Milano, 1936, p. 12, fig. 19; Brusin-Zovatto, *Monumenti Paleocristiani di Aquileia e Grado*, p. 513-522.

PLATE 67 - Detail of the Cesena missorium. The Cesena missorium is an exceptional product of late-ancient artistic movement in which the representational elements seen on the bottom of the dish appear to be linked in concept to the scene depicted along the rim. At the centre, the master of the house and his guests enjoy refreshment at the end of a day's hunting. The hunting scenes are illustrated on the border of the dish. Stately villas, small fenced-in buildings, trees and figures of birds provide the setting. A coin with the head of Theodosius, found at the same time as the dish, helps us at least to establish the date when the object was buried. Second half of 4th century A. D.

CESENA, Biblioteca Malatestiana (property of the State). — FROM CESENA, discovered in the local cemetery in 1948. — Bibliography: Arias F. A., III, 1950, n. 4431; id. B.d.D., p. 9; id., *Annuario Scuola Atene*, p. 309; *Ori Emilia*, n. 152.

Plate

PLATE 68 a - Two filigreed earrings of semicircular shape. Thin wires, both smooth and gadrooned, and circular globules complete the vivid decoration of this jewel. The technique and style are typically Byzantine. 6th — 7th centuries A. D. Height 1 ⁵/₈ ins; width 1 in.

> TARANTO, Museo Nazionale (inventory nos. 22619, 22520). — FROM OTRANTO, acquired by Capassa. — Bibliography: Breglia, *Japigia*, X, 1939, p. 36, fig. 24.

PLATE 68 b - Detail of a small gold cross which originally hung from a necklace. Engraved in the centre is the Virgin; below and at the sides are the busts of three Apostles. The inscription above is Greek. 7th century A. D.

> PALERMO, Museo Nazionale (catalogue no. 44). — FROM CAMPOBELLO DI MAZARA. — Bibliography: Salinas, *op. cit.*

PLATE 69 - Large silver fibula, partly coated with gold. The motif of a *cloisonné* cross-shaped rosette is repeated in the upper part and inside the lozenge in the lower half. Eleven lantern-shaped spokes protrude from the head of the jewel, and the lower end represents the stylized head of an ox. 7th century A. D. Length 4 ⁷/₈ ins; maximum width 2 ⁵/₈ ins.

> IMOLA, Museo Civico. — FROM IMOLA, podere "La Cardinale". — Bibliography: Undset, *Z. f. E.*, p. 23-24, fig. 14; Piani, *Museo di Imola*, p. 10; Werner, *Longobard*. Fibeln, p. 24, pl. XXVII, A 97; *Ori Emilia*, n. 222, fig. 65.

Plate 68 a

Plate 68 b

Plate 69

PLATE 71 a - The special importance attached to jewelry by the Lombards and particularly the status value of all ornaments of that period are accurately reflected by these large discs — worn as brooches — with a button or precious stone in the centre. Here the metal is decorated with filigreed motifs and the stones are set by the *cloisonné* technique. 7th century A. D. Diameter 2 ⁵/₈ ins.

ROME, Museo dell'Alto Medioevo. — FROM CASTEL TROSINO, Tomb no. 177. — Bibliography: Mengarelli, *Castel Trosino*, p. 324, pl. XIV, 6; Rademacher, *Fränkische Goldscheibenfibeln*, p. 43, fig. 5; Werner, *Langobard. Fibeln*, p. 38, c. 37, pl. XLIV; Becatti, n. 585.

PLATE 71 b - The barbaric practice of clothing the dead before burial in their most ostentatious garments and jewelry has contributed to the discovery of several products of that time. This ornamental disc is exhibitionist in the numerous colours and quantity of gold used. First half of 7th century A. D. Diameter 2 ⁵/₈ ins.

PARMA, Museo di Antichità. — FROM PARMA, found in 1950 in a tomb between Via della Repubblica and Via della Posta at a depth of some eight feet below street level. — Bibliography: *Ori Emilia*, n. 206, fig. 58-59, pl. I; Monaco, *Oreficeria Longobarda*, p. 19.

PLATE 70 - This ring of solid gold bears the image of Christ standing between two newly-weds. All around the border is a Greek inscription in niello. 7th century A. D. Diameter of ring ³/₄ in; diameter of seal ⁵/₈ in; weight 13 drams.

PALERMO, Museo Nazionale (catalogue no. 31 [R. E. 152]). — FROM SYRACUSE, probably found near the old arsenal, in the general area of ancient Byzantine baths. — Bibliography: Salinas, *Relazione del Real Museo di Palermo*, 1873, p. 57 ff., pl. A, I; Pace, *Sicilia Antica*, IV, p. 435 ff., same bibl.

Plate 70

Plate 71 a

Plate 71 b

PLATE 72 a - Strand of a necklace, consisting of beads of coral and vitreous paste, triangular pendants decorated with hammered buttons and single *bullae*. It is another heavy and ostentatious jewel such as barbaric women wore. 7th century A. D. Total length 9 ⁷/₈ ins.

ROME, Museo dell'Alto Medioevo. — FROM CASTEL TROSINO, Tomb no. 7. — Bibliography: Mengarelli, *Castel Trosino*, pl. VI, n. 2, c. 75-76; n. 6, 7, 8; Jenny-Volbach, *Germanischer Schmuck*, pl. XXI, n. 2; Becatti, n. 577.

PLATE 72 b - Gold fly. The body is laminated and the six legs are tightly twisted. 9th century A. D. Length ⁵/₈ in.

TRAPANI, Museo Pepoli (inventory no. 5015). — FROM ERICE.

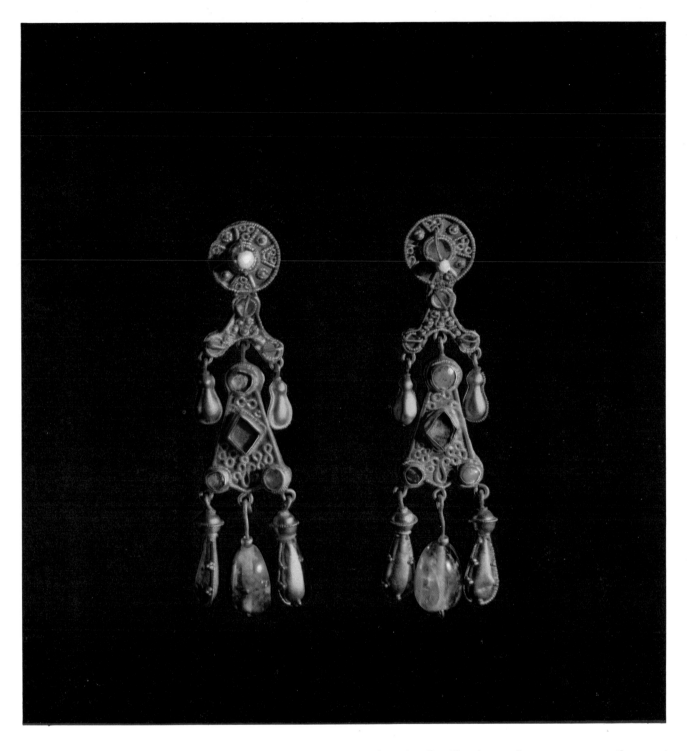

PLATE 73 - The objects found at Castel Trosino, in the Marche region, are among the most important discoveries of their kind, in that they throw a particularly interesting light on the Lombard rule, civilization and socio-political influence over the whole Italian peninsula. These earrings with pendants are vividly decorated with gold globules and amethysts. The upper parts of the two jewels are filigreed and adorned with pearls. 7th century A. D. Length 3 ⁷/₈ ins.

ROME, Museo dell'Alto Medioevo. — FROM CASTEL TROSINO. — Bibliography: Mengarelli, *Castel Trosino*, c. 65-66, pl. VI, 7; Aberg, *Goten*, p. 84, fig. 138; Becatti, n. 588.

Plate 75

PLATE 74 - The propagation of Christianity brought the symbols of that religion into jewelry. This typically Greek Cross is bordered with an entwined motif and decorated inside with hammered heads. Height 3 ⁵/₈ ins; width 3 ³/₈ ins;

BOLOGNA, Museo Civico. — Bibliography: Orsi, in *Atti Mem. Romagna*, 1883, p. 380, n. 80; Fuchs, *Langobard, Goldblattkreuze*, p. 94, pl. XXXIV; *Ori Emilia*, n. 319.

PLATE 75 a - Ornaments have been found not only in the tombs of barbaric women, but also in those of their warriors: gold and silver armour, swords and saddle ornaments such as this one from Castel Trosino. It is decorated with hammered geometrical motifs; tendrils, stylized griffins, and feline figures. 7th century A. D. Length of main piece 7 ³/₈ ins; length of two smaller pieces 1 ⁷/₈ ins.

ROME, Museo dell'Alto Medioevo. — FROM CASTEL TROSINO, Tomb no. 119. — Bibliography: Mengarelli, *Castel Trosino*, n. 1, c. 138, 139, pl. XIII; Aberg, *Goten*, p. 123, fig. 261; Jenni-Volbach, *Germanischer Schmuck*, n. 1, pl. XIX; Becatti, n. 556.

PLATE 75 b - In some parts of Italy, Lombard motifs from North and Central Europe became blended with Byzantine elements. This richly decorated sword from Castel Trosino has a typically Byzantine U-shaped hilt. The pierced decoration technique is also Byzantine.

ROME, Museo dell'Alto Medioevo. — FROM CASTEL TROSINO (Ascoli Piceno), Tomb F. — Bibliography: Mengarelli, *Castel Trosino*, c. 53, pl. V, 8; Aberg, *Goten*, p. 101, fig. 161; Jenny Volbach, *Germanischer Schmuck*, pl. XIX; Becatti, n. 218.

Plate 75

PLATE 76 - Two identical fibulae of gold and enamel in the shape of eagles. The eye of each bird consists of a crystal globe pierced in the centre and inset to represent the pupil. 5th — 6th centuries A. D. 1 $^7/_8$ ins.

> ROME, Musei Capitolini. — FROM ROME, found in 1888 in a burial ground on the Via Flaminia in the area of San Valentino. — Bibliography: De Rossi, in *Bull. Com.*, XXII, 1894, p. 158, pls. VII - VIII; Cecchelli, *La vita di Roma nel medioevo*, 1951, p. 888; Fuchs. *Langobard Goldblattkreuze*, p. 97.

PLATE 77 a - The motif of this necklace consists of prismatic emerald roots alternating with two small pearls. This jewel is evidence of the priority given to the chromatic element by Byzantine jewelers. Length 14 $^5/_8$ ins.

> SYRACUSE, Museo Archeologico Nazionale (inventory no. 53402). — FROM MISSORIA (Enna), accidentally discovered in a woman's tomb on September 1, 1953. — Bibliography: Gentili, *Not. Sc.*, 1954, p. 403.

PLATE 77 b - A further important discovery took place at Senise, near Potenza — on the reverse of these two earrings appears the seal of Heraclius and Tiberius, which implies the date as approximately 659-668 A. D. There is here an obvious similarity to the mosaic technique, and even an anticipation of paintedglass. The delicate female head is inscribed inside a circle divided into twelve cavities with small red stones inserted into each. End of 7th century A. D. Length 2 $^3/_8$ ins.

> NAPLES, Museo Archeologico Nazionale. — FROM SENISE. — Bibliography: *Not. Sc.*, 1916, p. 329; Breglia, n. 996-997, pl. XLII, I, 1; Siviero, n. 533, pls. CCXLIX - CCLIV.

Plate 76

Plate 7

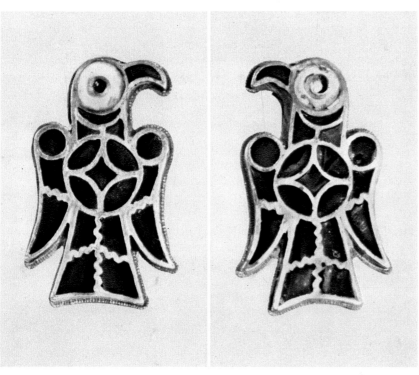

Plate 7

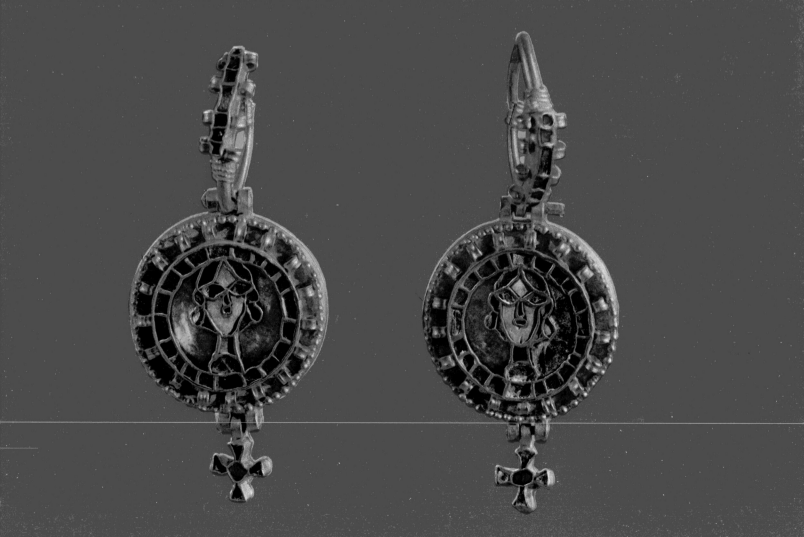

PLATE 78 - Buckle of a sword-belt, with mobile prong. Every inch of this silver ornament is minutely carved and chiselled. The *horror vacui* of the early Etruscans was now reappearing in the history of jewelry. Length 5 ⁷/₈ ins; width 2 ³/₄ ins.

FORLI, Museo Civico. — Bibliography: *Ori Emilia*, n. 235.

PLATE 79 - Other important discoveries of Lombard jewelry were made in the general area of Nocera Umbra. This arched silver fibula with a heart-shaped centre is decorated with punched motifs along the border and inside the upper plate. The lower part is fashioned in the shape of a stylized boar's head. 6th — 7th centuries A. D. Length 6 ³/₄ ins.

ROME, Museo dell'Alto Medioevo. — FROM NOCERA UMBRA, Tomb no. 23. — Bibliography: Pasqui-Paribeni, *Nocera Umbra*, c. 208, fig. 60; Aberg, *Goten*, p. 69, fig. 106; Werner, *Langobard. Fibeln*, A. 95-96, pl. XXVI, p. 23, 24; Becatti, n. 552 a, b.

Plate 78

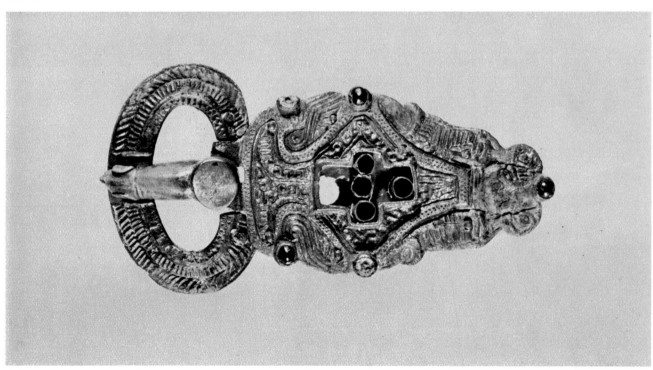

Plate 79

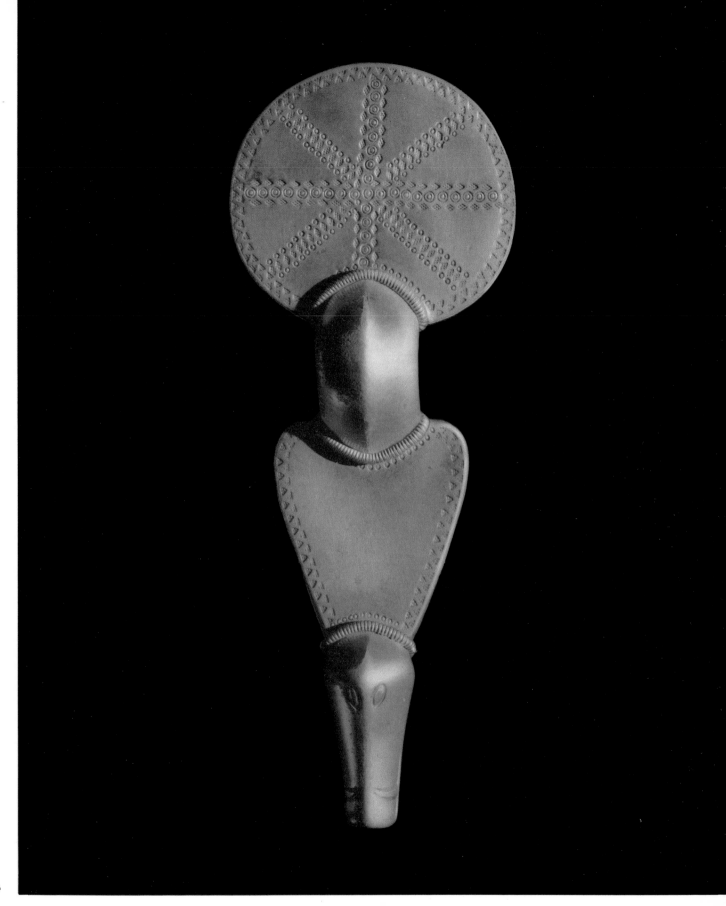

Plate 80

PLATE 80 - Ornaments such as these were frequently put inside Barbaric tombs to enhance the richness of the deceased's clothing. The usual decorative vividness, echoing Byzantine and Germanic motifs, is visible in the filigreed finish of the objects. 7th century A. D. Length 1 ⁵/₈ ins. and 1 ³/₈ ins.

ROME, Museo dell'Alto Medioevo. — FROM CASTEL TROSINO. — Bibliography: Mengarelli, *Castel Trosino*, pl. V, n. 9, col. 143, n. 19, fig. 171, pl. V, n. 7, col. 141, 142, n. 15, fig. 167; Becatti, n. 568 a-b, n. 571 a, b, c.

PLATE 81 - The acceptance of the Christian faith by the Lombards is reflected in this typical example of their craft: a cross of gold lamina with arms of equal length. This splendid example, found at Cividale, was decorated with eight heads, portrayed frontally, and set with nine stones: 1 Oriental garnet, 4 lapislazuli and 4 aquamarines. Third or fourth decade of 7th century A. D. Length of arms 4 ³/₈ x 4 ³/₈ ins.

CIVIDALE DEL FRIULI, Museo Archeologico Nazionale (inventory no. 168). — FROM CIVIDALE. — Bibliography: Cecchelli, *Mon. de Friuli*, Rizzoli 1943, p. 205 ff.

80

Plate 81

INDEX
OF
TEXT AND
ILLUSTRATIONS

84

COLOUR PLATES

THIS BOOK WAS PRINTED AND BOUND
BY STABILIMENTO D'ARTE GRAFICHE
DI AMILCARE PIZZI, MILAN